BEER BITES

BEER BITES

Tasty Recipes and Perfect Pairings for Brew Lovers

Christian DeBenedetti & Andrea Slonecker

FOREWORD BY Eric Asimov

PHOTOGRAPHS BY John Lee

CHRONICLE BOOKS

SAN FRANCISCO

Library of Congress Cataloging-in-Publication
Data available.

ISBN 978-1-4521-3524-3

Manufactured in China

Designed by Alice Chau
Photography by John Lee
Food styling by Lillian Kang
Prop styling by Christine Wolheim

10 9 8 7 6 5 4 3 2 1

Chronicle Books LLC
680 Second Street
San Francisco, California 94107
www.chroniclebooks.com

To my mom, Ellen, who taught me to love cooking, eating, and drinking, and who always said: If you can picture it, you can pull it off.

—Christian

To my dad, Steve, for offering me my first taste of beer if I'd grab him one out of the fridge.

—Andrea

CONTENTS

FOREWORD

Aside from its obvious virtues, beer is one of the most versatile and intriguing beverages to match with food. Yet the clear potential of food-and-beer pairing has been woefully underexplored.

Fine restaurants may pay occasional lip service to beer, but when it's time to recommend what goes best with their food they focus on the far more profitable wine list. Great beer is most cherished in taverns and pubs. There, the standards for beer service may be exacting but the food too often tends toward fraternity fare—dessicated burgers, frozen prefabricated pretzels with the texture of plastic foam, stringy fried mozzarella sticks, gloppy wings. Pitiful excuses for pub grub.

The United States has come a long way in understanding that beer can be complex and fascinating. The next step in treating beer with the respect it deserves is to make sure it is surrounded by great food. Enter Christian DeBenedetti and Andrea Slonecker. Their new book, *Beer Bites*, does exactly that.

I know both Christian and Andrea by their previous works. Christian's book *The Great American Ale Trail* is a brilliant guide to finding great beer all around the country. And with Andrea's book *Pretzel Making at Home*, I conquered my own fears to achieve a long-nurtured ambition of baking great soft pretzels myself. She has a rare talent for simplifying seemingly complicated tasks. Together, they strike just the right tone: knowledgeable and authoritative but easygoing. They understand that cooking, eating, and drinking are joyful acts. Fear of making mistakes has no place here.

"Relax. Beer is not wine," they write, to which I say, "What a relief!" The pairing of food and beverage is a practical skill, borne of experience. The more you do it, the more instinctive it becomes as you discover what works and what does not, what you like and what you don't. Yet, so many guides to food-and-wine pairing turn it into a hard-and-fast, anxiety-ridden procedure full of arcane rules and complicated charts. With *Beer Bites*, pairing becomes instead an enjoyable journey on which nothing goes wrong because you learn something every time.

Beer Bites does not fall into the trap of over-specificity. It's not the hint of coriander that makes all the difference in selecting a proper accompaniment, but the overall sense of a dish. Let the professionals fuss over whether a poppy-seed bun rather than a sesame bun dramatically changes the sort of beer you want to go with your burger. Home cooks require more general guidelines, which Christian and Andrea understand and provide.

Instead of adhering to hidebound definitions of beer styles, Christian and Andrea recognize that twenty-first-century brewers all over the world have blended traditions to forge new types of beers. They draw up broader categories for beer that require simple common sense to understand rather than rote memorization, and then offer a range of recommendations for each dish.

The recipes draw deeply from global beer cultures. Some may appear daunting—drunken chicken hearts, anyone?—but most play with established forms and turn them into altogether new and enticing dishes.

Playful, down-to-earth, unpretentious, encouraging—this is the beer-and-food book that you didn't know you needed but now can't do without.

—Eric Asimov

INTRODUCTION

What would life be without beer? Wait—let's not go there. Too depressing. A better question is, what would beer be without food? You may have an answer in mind, but this is not a book about going without. This is a book about combining the joys of the tap with those of the table, in ways that will seem both familiar and, we hope, surprising. When we set out to write this book, we really had no idea where the ingredients would take us, or where the beers would take us, or, most of all, how those bites and beers might travel together to a third destination, hard to describe—a certain sort of sensory heaven.

Sometimes we're inspired to cook at home; sometimes we gather with friends. Often we reach for a beer in there somewhere. But how often do we match pints and plates intentionally? We are not the first to say that while pairing cuisine with wine is an age-old pursuit, it's time for beer pairing to catch up. Where it arrives, though, is likely a different place—not one with starched white tablecloths, piped-in classical piano, and solicitous waiters carrying silver platters and scraping crumbs out of sight. No, beer's best place seems a lot more like a room full of weathered wood tables, fireplaces, friends, maybe a fiddle. The culture of drinking beer with food at home is as ancient as agriculture itself; beer, brewed communally for both sustenance and celebration, originates from the farm, the fields, the hearth and home. Scores of culinary traditions survive and thrive reflecting the inclusion of beer at the dining table across the ages.

There are also new traditions coming to life as beer evolves and styles morph across continents. Until recently, it seems even home cooks with a passion for beer have had little inspiration when it comes to thoughtful pairings. We've been winging it.

We needn't any longer. Thanks to ambitious brewers and beer-championing chefs who appreciate the intensely satisfying ways that beer and food can work together in the dining experience, a "beer table" consciousness is coming to life, or back to life, around the world. Michelin-starred chefs curating sold-out beer dinners with barrel-aged rarities? Check. Gastropubs with deep, lovingly curated beer lists in city centers and secret corners? Check. World-class, top-ranked restaurants commissioning house beers from "nomad" or "gypsy" brewers, the pop-up chefs of brewdom? Check.

To shape this cookbook, we rolled up our sleeves and started with the classics—recipes from regions around the world with longstanding beer traditions. We did this with the goal of leading a deeper and more informed exploration of the interplay between beer and food. From there, we got creative, dreaming up dishes inspired by urban street carts; new-era innovators; and our own half-mad stove-top tinkering, with fifteen bottles of beer open on the counter. Within these pages, you can step into our Beer Bites kitchen, equal parts huge hoppy experiment and potential roadmap for your own tests and tastings. Our hope is that you'll be inspired to open a good bottle of brew and cook something that accentuates its unique taste, creating an experience beyond just drinking a beer.

As mentioned, we want this book to launch fun, flavorful explorations of your own. So choose a few recipes (how about a theme night?), procure some beers, and let the experiments begin. Who knows, you might just have the most fun ever eating and drinking beer.

Now can we taste some beer, please?

METHODOLOGY

There are books that explain, in Byzantine detail, the differences between established beer styles. That is not our bailiwick here. Whatever the starting point—a beer style, an ingredient, a flavor group—we were aiming to create broad, experimental guidelines rather than some sort of rigid *diktat* to follow. We set out to have some serious fun in the kitchen and to bring you a record of our journey. Our end goal: Exciting, delicious, easy-to-follow recipes, with recommendations and information about what to drink with them. We collected and sampled hundreds of beers, testing and retesting dishes whose flavors would elevate, and be elevated by, some of the best brews in the world.

Our aim was to make a cookbook for beer lovers and a food lover's guide to great beer. It is neither an encyclopedia of beer styles nor a textbook on the history and food chemistry of bratwurst. The methodology is, was, and should be, for you. Does the combination taste good? If so, have more. If not, what's the next beer we can try?

You might not agree with our picks. Trainspotters may notice that we include only certain beer styles, not the entire gamut of hundreds we could have attempted to cram in. But this is not a beer puzzle, a game of Tetris won only after the last beer style in the world has a food pairing. It's intended as a lively and loving study of beers and their flavors, and the foods that bring them alive. The more than three hundred beers of about forty varying styles mentioned in this book are all, simply, great with food; some have amazing powers of versatility, matching many flavors from simple to complex (see chapter 4); and some are a little more ornery, requiring rather exacting flavor palates (see chapter 3).

It's not about style. Well, actually, it is about style. But even more than that, it's about flavor.

During our research, we came across an important article by our friend, Washington D.C.–based brewer, publican, and restaurateur Greg Engert, which presents beer styles according to broad flavor groups instead of rigid, geographical, historical "rules." This is a brilliant, helpful approach (cheers, Greg), because, when it comes down to it, flavor is more important than a fixation on styles. Flavor is the path to pleasure, whereas styles represent accepted traditions, rules, goalposts, "norms." Obviously the concept of beer styles—widely credited to the late British beer writer Michael Jackson, the first writer to identify and describe them in any meaningful, public way—is central to brewing and beer appreciation. But today it's possible to talk about beer in broader terms, too. Inspired by Engert's methodology, we've broken down—in our own way—the wide range of beer varieties into groups divided by flavors and how they are experienced with various foods. One very important reason for this: Beer styles are no longer quite as codified as they once were. American hops are showing up in Scandinavian farmhouse ales. Dutch brewers are tweaking English bitters. Belgian masters are having a whack at American IPA. Saisons are pouring out jet-black and hopped with new experimental varieties. And brewers in Texas and Alaska are replicating fermentation methods once thought possible only in a small patch of Belgian countryside. As methods swirl and evolve, so too do beer flavors. It's a beautiful thing.

In other words, we begin this book with "crisp and clean" beers and bites rather than "German-style Pilsners" that you must drink only with *spätzle*. Next we tackle a spectrum of "fruit and spice" flavors, then "hoppy and herbal," followed by "sour and complex." In the last two chapters, we revel in running the "malty, rich, and sweet" and "deep, roasty, and smoky" gamuts. All the way through, we present easy-to-execute recipes that go way beyond typical greasy pub grub.

Within these chapters, you'll discover fresh ideas in the beer-food discussion, with recipes such as Grilled Eggplant Rolls with Cucumber Labneh (page 150), Mussels in Celery-Gueuze Cream (page 100), and a Fruit Beer Float (page 64). Old World classics from Belgium, Germany, England, and other beer-loving societies are rediscovered in dishes like Raspberry Liège Waffles (page 62), those classic Bamberg Onions (page 148), and English Bitter Ale Fish and Chips (page 85). Each recipe is partnered not only with a short list of attainable bottled beers to seek out—both Old World and new—but also a detailed introduction, including details from brewing science for both experts and the uninitiated, and engaging commentary on how and why a beer's flavors work so well with the dish from a cultural, culinary, and/or historical perspective.

BREWERS' TOOLKIT

Whether you're a seasoned home brewer or complete newcomer, it's helpful to be reminded of the birds and the bees of beers. The process is straightforward: The brewer obtains malted grains, steeps them in very hot water to make a "mash," and then boils that runoff with hop flowers in various forms for anywhere from one to five hours, style depending. The "wort" (pronounced "wert") is cooled to a comfortable temperature for yeast, which is then "pitched" in, and the fermentation process begins shortly after. Some days later (three or four on up for ales; up to four weeks or more for many lagers), the yeast has chewed up the sugars in the cooled wort, creating alcohol and CO_2 and expelling heat. The remaining alcohol content, or %ABV (alcohol by volume; that is, simply the percentage of the total volume of the liquid that is alcohol), tells you how "hot" (basically, boozy) a given beer might be. After an optional period of con-ditioning (resting, really), and other processes such as filtration and blending, the beer is ready to be packaged in kegs, bottles, or cans.

INGREDIENTS

The myriad flavors, textures, and taste perceptions of beer come from this alchemy of malt, hops, water, and yeast, and the manner of their combination: the brewing process. Grains of every strain impart the malty flavors and sweetness underlying so many beers, while hops affect aroma, flavor, and, perhaps most actively, the bitter elements. The minerals in and alkalinity of the water source are elemental to the mouthfeel, and any bitterness and the overall flavor, too. Yeast overlays the beer with aromatics, lending unique character to the various styles of beer, from clean, bready lagers to fruity ales and "barnyard" wild ales. An array of spices, fruits, and other assorted fermentable additions (such as Belgian candi sugar, squash, molasses, or honey) contribute deeper complexity to scores of beers around the world.

HOPS

Hops (*Humulus lupulus*), a plant with resinous, pale green flowers that grow on vines, come in dozens of commercial varieties. First used in the Middle Ages, beer just wouldn't be what it is without them. (There are some hopless beers, called *gruits*, that can be interesting, but none of them made the cut for this book.) Harvested in fall and boiled with malted, roasted, and milled grains that have been steeped in hot water, hops impart both bitterness and aroma, depending on the variety and when the brewer adds them (early for an emphasis on bitterness; late for more interest in the aromatic qualities). The possible nuances derived from the many types of hops include delicately spicy, pungent, minty, citrusy, piney, tropical, herbaceous, woody, limelike, weedlike (yes, as in Mary Jane), and, in the ever-more-popular Citra and Simcoe varieties, musky or catty, as in redolent of cat spray (although, if it can be imagined, not unpleasant, just as it is with certain German and New Zealand white wines, like Sauvignon Blanc. For the chemistry-minded, the culprit is a sulfur compound called p-menthane-8-thiol-3-one). Integral to beer, they also affect head retention and act as a preservative. Hops come mainly from Germany, the Czech Republic, and the Pacific Northwest.

Hops contribute to:

- aroma
- bitterness
- aftertaste
- head retention

THREE HOPS TO DROP IN CONVERSATION

CASCADE The piney, grapefruit-pithy flavor of these flowers drives American pale ale and IPA lovers to distraction. Similar popular hops used in many IPAs include Simcoe and Amarillo.

HALLERTAUER This is one of the most famous so-called noble German hops, noted for their delicate properties and mild aromas. The notes they deliver have been described as slightly fruity and/or spicy; flowery; earthy; and haylike. Hallertauer are found in many German lagers. Compare to Saaz; Tettnanger.

NELSON SAUVIN Said to be named in part for Sauvignon Blanc wine, this New Zealand variety smells unmistakably of passion fruit. Found in many new-school American and Belgian pale ales and IPAs. Compare to Motueka; Riwaka.

MALT

Malted barley (*Hordeum vulgare*) is the most common base for beer, and has been used in brewing since the reigns of ancient Egyptians, Chinese, and Sumerians. It's produced by wetting the grain with water to make it sprout, and then drying it to arrest the germination. During this process, enzymes transform the sprouted grain's starches into sugars that yeast will thrive on. The malted barley imparts color and body, as well as the alcohol formed during fermentation. Try some of the dried grain next time you visit a homebrew shop; it's a bit like munching on Grape-Nuts. Brewers also use wheat, oats, rye, sorghum, spelt, and many other malted grains. If you've wondered why the beer you are drinking is pale and light-bodied or jet-black and coffee-like, the answer is in the malt.

Malt contributes to:

- sweetness and alcohol levels, depending on the strain of grain used and the length of fermentation
- body and mouthfeel, in the form of proteins
- color (100 percent of a beer's color is due to the malt—the longer the roasting time, the darker the beer)

THREE BREWERS' MALTS TO KNOW

AMERICAN TWO-ROW Light, clean, versatile, and smooth, this pale barley malt can be used as the base for nearly every beer style.

CHOCOLATE MALT Highly roasted. Rich, dark color, with hints of black coffee and bittersweet chocolate; found in stout, porter, and all sorts of brown ales.

PILSNER MALT Made from European two-row barley. A strong, sweet malt flavor. Used as the base for Pilsner, obviously, but also many saisons, bières de garde, and other European brews.

YEAST

Simply put, yeasts are the single-cell creatures responsible for fermenting all beer. The careful management of these active cultures diverges in two main directions: warm-active, top-fermenting processes, responsible for ales; and the cold-working, bottom-settling process that delivers us our beloved, clean, crisp lagers. Each signature strain takes on "house character." Wild yeasts depart from all the playbooks entirely, which is why so many brewers fear and love them in equal measure. Every sour beer uses some sort of wild yeast, whether it's a strain somewhat tamed in labs, one harvested from the skins of fruit, or a yeast captured straight out of the air itself—the wildest there is.

Yeast contributes to:

- alcohol levels
- spice, flavor, and "bite"
- esters

THREE YEASTS TO THE WIND

ALE YEAST *Saccharomyces cerevisiae* This yeast may have come from the skins of ancient grapes. Hardy and hungry, this is the critter who gives countless beers (and baked goods) their mojo. It is active at warmer temperatures, and (bonus!) rich in B vitamins. Ale beers include golden ales; English bitter and Extra Special Bitter; pale ales; India pale ales; ambers; browns; stouts; and all manner of Belgian brews.

LAGER YEAST *Saccharomyces pastorianus*, formerly known as *S. carlsbergensis* This is the yeast that changed the world when it was isolated circa 1842, allowing brewers to "lager," or cold-store, beers for longer periods of time, resulting in clean, bready flavors and "brite"—that is, crystal clear—beers. Used in Pilsners, German lagers, bocks, American pale lagers, and many other styles.

WILD YEAST *Brettanomyces* Yeasts in the genus of "Brett" (as brewers call it) can impart earthy, leathery, barnyardy, funky, tart, angular flavors to beers. Some are so voracious, they will eat into oak barrels. Similarly, some skilled brewers ferment beer with the help of certain strains of beer-friendly bacteria (*Lactobacillus, Pediococcus*). If you love sourdough, Greek yogurt, funky cheeses, and other complex foods, chances are you'll love sour beers made with wild yeast, such as lambic, gueuze, gose, kriek, faro, Berliner weisse, and various American wild ales.

WATER

It seems obvious enough, but the importance of this foundation for fine beers cannot be overstated: Brewers *obsess* on water quality. What matters is not only purity but the ionic and nutritional payload (or lack thereof) of minerals, metals, and the pH factor. You could spend a lifetime studying the organic chemistry of water and how it affects the end product in beer craft.

BEER STYLES FLAVOR CHEAT SHEET

When you think about beer in terms of style, unless you have a vast, encyclopedic memory for minute style distinctions, it can be easy to get lost in the details. That's why with *Beer Bites*, we set out to create more than a cookbook with beer pairings but an exploration of *flavor*—in beers, naturally, and in the delicious plates following.

What you'll find in this book is far different from what you might find in brewing text-books. There's a fair amount of subjectivity in styles these days as they morph and change. One person's Belgian tripel is another's strong golden ale. Ditto for American pale ale and the hot "session" IPA category—really, what's the difference? Another's imperial porter is someone else's stout. This kind of hair splitting goes on and on. Regional alle-giances and influences deepen the mystery. Some beers are known by one style but exhibit the typical flavors—intense fruitiness, say—of others. And, of course, there are sub-styles of the divisions of character-stics we settled on for the following cheat sheet, and the chapters that organize this book. But like we said, this is an unscientific, subjective, highly improvisational road-map to fun and flavor, not a thesis. It's probably time to open a beer. Do you have a beer open yet? There, good.

CRISP & CLEAN

PILSNER: pale, dry, bitter, crisp, faintly malty

HELLES: golden, light, crisp, refreshing, bready

KÖLSCH: pale, faintly sweet, not bitter, quenching

AMERICAN PALE LAGER: light-bodied, faintly sweet, cold

VIENNA PALE LAGER: caramel-hued, faintly bitter, bready

KELLERBIER: bitter, refreshing, cloudy, buttery, fulsome

CREAM ALE: light, faintly sweet, not bitter, easy

INDIA PALE LAGER: pale, clean, bready; citrus, lemon

DRY IRISH STOUT: light, dry, tangy, refreshing; cocoa

FRUIT & SPICE

GOSE: light, salty, sour, spicy, complex; coriander

WITBIER: light, bright, fruity, mineral; coriander, orange peel

HEFEWEIZEN: medium-bodied, effervescent, cloudy, spicy; clove

RYE BEER: reddish, assertive, stronger, vibrant, spicy

STRONG PEACH ALE: ripe, summery, strong; peach

WEIZENBOCK: strong, clean, malty, bready, spicy

SOUR/FRUIT ALE: fresh, intense, tart, fruity, complex

HOPPY & HERBAL

ENGLISH BITTER: bronze-hued, mild, biscuity, soft

PALE ALE: copper-hued, flowery, tangy, bright; melon

AMERICAN IPA: dry, assertive, tangy, pungent, flowery; pine

BELGIAN PALE ALE: efferves-cent, earthy, spicy, aromatic, flowery

BELGIAN IPA: bitter, long, pungent, musty, earthy

WHITE IPA: bright, bitter, faintly sweet, juicy, tangy; coriander

IMPERIAL IPA: tropical, biscuity; pine, peach, apricot, citrus rind, marmalade

EXTRA SPECIAL BITTER (ESB): full-bodied, bitter, bready, tangy; shortcake

SOUR & COMPLEX

SAISON & FARMHOUSE ALE: mineral; grass, hay, apricot, bitter greens

LAMBIC: deep, tangy; basement, barnyard, funk, cheese, stone fruit, lemon

GUEUZE: sparkling, bright, angular, mineral, intense

FRUIT LAMBIC: sweet or dry, tart; stone fruit, leather, tannins

FLANDERS RED: bright berry red, tart, lively, vinous; oak, cherry

FLANDERS BROWN/OUD BRUIN: sweet-sour; tobacco, malt, raisin, cherry

STRONG BELGIAN DARK: rich; toffee, treacle, coffee, molasses

MALTY, RICH & SWEET

MÄRZEN: copper-hued, mild, juicy, bready, spicy; caramel

BIÈRE DE GARDE: amber-hued, soft, dry, malty

BROWN ALE: medium-bodied, soft, faintly sweet, nutty

LONDON PORTER: dark, roasted; caramel, chocolate

OATMEAL STOUT: light-bodied, roasted, silky, soft; coffee

OLD ALE/STOCK ALE: deep, sherry-like; caramel, raisin

ABBEY DUBBEL: rich, spicy, complex; caramel, cocoa

ABBEY TRIPEL: pale, sweet, fruity, boozy, fluffy; banana

BELGIAN STRONG GOLDEN ALE: golden, bittersweet, malty, peppery

QUADRUPEL: spicy, boozy; plum, cherry, brown sugar

BARLEYWINE: powerful, fruity; toffee, coffee, vanilla, wood

DEEP, ROASTY & SMOKY

AMERICAN PORTER: dark brown, tangy, roasted; coffee

RAUCHBIER-HELLES: crisp, refreshing, smoky, bready

MAPLE PORTER: deep brown, rich, syrupy, indulgent

GRÄTZER/LICHTENHAINER: light, sour, wheaty, smoky

SCHWARZBIER: black, light, tangy, clean, dry, roasted

RAUCHBIER: spicy, smoky, malty; campfire, creosote, caramel

DOPPELBOCK: caramel, toffee, treacle, espresso, chocolate cake

STOUT: bitter, juicy, astringent, thin, roasted; espresso

IMPERIAL BELGIAN BROWN: roasted; molasses, caramel, earth

IMPERIAL STOUT: viscous; espresso, oak, wood, stone fruit

COFFEE STOUT: rich, bitter, astringent; iced coffee

BOURBON BARREL-AGED IMPERIAL STOUT: vanilla, toffee, espresso, black cherry, dark chocolate

THE FIVE TASTES AND HOW THEY RELATE TO BEER AND FOOD

Scientists have identified (and still actively debate) the five basic tastes to which the human tongue is sensitive. Those tastes, in combination with aromas sensed by the nose, are what make magical things happen when beer and food collide. Here's a simple primer on the five elements of taste as they play out in the arena of beer.

SWEET

Sweetness in beer comes from barley malt, and occasionally adjuncts such as molasses, Belgian candi sugars, and other sweet fermentables. It creates and contrasts with alcohol, and punctuates hop bitterness in the beer itself. Sweet, malty flavors in beer often complement those same flavors found in desserts, but also rich, bready, or caramelized savory bites. Fried foods, baked goods, warming spices, deep fruit glazes, browned vegetables, funky cheeses, and rich sauces are all complemented by sweetness in beer.

SOUR

Acidity is a welcome characteristic in a family of beers that includes Belgian krieks, lambics, and gueuzes; American and Flemish sour ales; and German gose and Berliner weisse. Their flavorful tang is the result of wild yeasts and bacteria (akin to those found in good Greek yogurt and other probiotic-rich foods). Lighter sour beers can serve as perfect aperitifs, while heavier versions are best enjoyed with food. The fuller and more sour the brew, the more this is true—their virtues lie in contrasts. For one, the acidity of full-bodied sour beers scrubs fattiness from the tongue, a powerful, appetizing effect. And as Michael Tonsmeire points out in his book *American Sour Beers*, the melanoidins in dark sour beers mirror the melanoidins produced from searing meat, making them a reliable choice with a steak. Even briny seafoods can set up intriguing contrasts. In some sour beers with aromas akin to earth and leather imparted by *Brettanomyces* yeast, umami (see right) comes to the fore.

SALTY

There are few actual salty beers (among the exceptions are the gose beers in chapter 2), but saltiness in food makes for one of the most important, and common, pairing interactions. Perhaps it's some beers' higher calling to quench the thirst that ensues after eating a salty French fry or grilled brat. Salty foods love beers, as evidenced by the salt-laden menus of pubs and beer halls throughout the world. Think about how the crunchy salt crystals on the outside of a soft pretzel are delightfully cleansed on the palate by a swig of cool brew.

BITTER

Bitterness, the signature taste of the beers discussed in chapter 3, can be quite a trick to match with food. But good, balanced hoppy beers turn out to be great with foods that feature one of the other four tastes in an equally big way. Bitterness is brought into check by highly acidic foods and umami especially well, and a little sweetness and saltiness in a dish will alleviate some of the sting. In spicy dishes, hoppy, bitter beers first cool the palate, but can sometimes finish in a five-alarm fire and other times highlight the heat in a desirable way.

UMAMI

Umami is a taste perception that is difficult to describe. In simple terms, it is a deep savoriness, triggered by proteins in foods like Parmesan cheese, soy sauce, prosciutto, anchovies, fish sauce, shiitake mushrooms, long-cooked broths, miso, and even mangos. What *is* easy to define is how umami is enhanced by the other four basic tastes. Salt in particular is the crutch of umami, but that's a rarity in beer (just season your food well). So, we have sour, bitter, and sweet to work with—pretty much the big three of flavor foundations that you *do* find in beer, making foods high in umami the easiest beer pairings of all. Think chicken wings, baby back ribs, grilled sausages, and sushi rolls—maybe all are tried-and-true beer foods for that very reason.

Get the Good Stuff: Finding Craft Beer

The "good beer" revolution has brought Americans an unprecedented range of choice in the beer aisle. It can be completely overwhelming; beer selections change almost daily, and new breweries and venues for their products have opened, on average, at least once a day in recent years. The beers in this book, for the most part, are not industrial products. We sought out, in mid-2014, an array of the best and yet not *too* obscure beers to go with the companion recipes. Some came from the corner grocery convenience store (e.g., Guinness, Negra Modelo), others from bottle shops with more than a thousand selections (thank you, Portland, Oregon). With luck, you should be able to find most of them nearby (or, where legal, order them online).

Check your area for bottle shops advertising a wide selection of beers and pay a visit. If the beers aren't disorganized and dusty, you're off to a very good start. Read the labels for dates; sell-by and bottled-on stamps are becoming more popular. If you see, oh, six to ten Belgian beer brands, such as Orval, Rochefort, and Dupont, chances are you've come to a good place. Better yet, check online area guides for bottle shops catering to diehard beer aficionados. You might be surprised to find an incredible selection staffed by passionate beer lovers in your own backyard. Then, start asking questions. Hundreds, if not thousands, of good beer bottle shops have opened across the country in recent years. In Oregon, even gas stations sell craft beer. We're living in a golden age.

HOW TO PROPERLY TASTE BEER

To the question of what pace you should apply to the tasting of new beers, to best develop your palate for well-crafted products, there is a very practical (and happy) answer: Often. While you don't want to confuse your impressions, the best way to learn about beer and how all its flavors and nuances play across your senses is to drink it—in moderation, of course—and taste it while you drink it, all the time. Every day, even. And while you are treating yourself to this studied pleasure, keep the following things in mind.

POUR

Beer should normally be poured straight into the middle of a very clean, room-temperature glass (more on that later; see facing page), forming a healthy head in the process. Put your foam anxieties aside—a head of anywhere from ½ in/12 mm to 3 in/7.5 cm is perfectly proper. The head is an integral part of experiencing the best of a beer, not just a visual treat or proof that the beer isn't flat—the head expresses aroma and, of course, contributes to mouthfeel, a sense of body or roundness. Some styles, like saisons and tripels, throw a glorious, meringue-like head. Yum.

A note on beer bottled with corks and wire-cage enclosures. Beers re-fermented in those bottles pack tremendous pressure. Do not shake them or point them at anyone, of course. And here's a tip: Throw a washcloth over the cork once you've unwired it. Grip the cork with one hand, gently turn the bottle in the other, and release the cork with a smooth "*fssss*" rather than a loud "*pok*." If it foams—and they do sometimes—set it in the sink. If it gushes for more than 20 seconds, you may have an infected bottle. Take it back.

SMELL

Relax. Beer is not wine. We love to say that beer isn't becoming more winelike, it's becoming more *beerlike*. Age-worthy, complex beers have been with us for centuries; it's just that merchants stopped selling them, and crassly marketed, flavorless macrobrews monopolized the shelves—until now. You should smell the bouquet of your beer. Inhale deeply at first meet, and develop a practice of drawing the beer's aromas through your nasal passages whenever you take a sip—something we may not do unless mindful of it. Ales have more aroma, but lagers aren't devoid of a profile you can get to know. Extra points for getting foam on your nose.

TASTE

Let the beer flow over your entire tongue and swish it around in your mouth, but there's no need to go overboard, sucking air through the teeth and into the mouth as some do with wines. Sour taste receptors, major conductors of beer flavor, are found all over the tongue. Commonly perceived flavors in beer comprise an astonishing array: grain, biscuits, caramel, toffee, coffee, fruit, spice, molasses, cedar, oak, grapefruit, pine, lemongrass, currant, raisin, mint, straw, and espresso—to name a very few. Practice finding words for the flavors you're experiencing by drawing on your knowledge of food. Because, of course, beer *is* food.

SWALLOW

A point of pride: Beer lovers do not spit. Beer should be swallowed. Carbonation, which is also part of the experience of tasting beer, must be experienced with the whole palate, by taking a nice big taste and washing it over the entire tongue and into the belly.

REPEAT

Beer contains alcohol. Some clock in over 12% ABV. There's no harm in enjoying the tenth sip a bit more than the first. And so on. But keep in mind that inebriation, hot ovens, and sharp knives are a loser's combo. Don't get drunk before you broil the ribs glazed in Trappist-style quadrupel beer and marmalade (see page 130). You won't fully remember how insanely good they are.

HOW TO PROPERLY STORE BEER

Are you lucky enough to have a wine cellar? Congrats, you've got a beer cellar, too. But here's a little-known fact: Drink it fresh. All beer is ready to drink when it leaves the brewery. The leftover bottles of pale ale from last summer's BBQ? Pour them down the drain, and use that cellar to shelve your beer as soon as you bring it home. Beer should be stored in a cool, dark place or refrigerator at all times. Cans, now more common in the craft-beer world, are good vessels for keeping beer fresh, because they don't allow damaging sunlight to penetrate the container. Higher-alcohol beers have a longer shelf life; an ABV of 9% or so will keep for up to a few months, and precious few beers of 12 to 15% ABV and higher can age, deliciously, for decades. But life is short. Drink those beers you're keeping for a "special occasion" now, because you're likely to enjoy them far more now than when they've gone south.

SERVING TEMPERATURES

Here's a good, and very generalized, rule of thumb: Beers express their flavors best somewhere in the neighborhood of the temperature at which they were fermented and "conditioned," that is, settled down in tanks to clarify and get ready for packaging. Ales tend to ferment at room temperature, but condition in the brewery at around 55°F/13°C, and so could be opened straight from your cool basement, for example; lagers ferment at cooler temperatures, but certainly above freezing, say, 40 to 45°F/4 to 7°C, and so should be stored in the back of your fridge. These days, brewers often put recommended serving temperatures on their labels; this is a very helpful thing.

Note: It's nearly impossible to taste much of anything at ice-cold temperatures. Ironically, that's why cheap American canned beers are always depicted in the classic, even sexy, sweating buckets of ice. The ultimate rules of thumb: Apply cellar temperature for ales, including wild ales, and fridge temp for lagers (see above). But, have we dropped an ice cube in a beer before? Maybe!

A Note on Glassware

We're not *too* fussy on glassware. It absolutely affects beer and how we taste it, but starting out, you don't need to go out and spend a fortune. Instead, build a collection slowly; use what you have for now. To standardize our results, and to appear in control (to ourselves) for three months locked in a kitchen with enough beer to drop an elephant, we sampled almost all of the hundreds of beers we tried out of small, beakerlike chemistry cups. The most important thing is cleanliness; a dirty glass destroys a beer's head, rendering the brewer's work null and void. Also, yuck.

The same yuck is true of frozen pint glasses. With the possible exception of very cheap, pale American lagers purchased three dozen at a time, maybe while standing at a sports bar for the big game, we do not recommend them. The frozen tumblers absorb freezer odors, kill head retention, and begin to sweat, often slimily, as soon as you pour a beer. (Think about the acrid, sweaty air inside bars that is cooled and pumped into the AC units that chill glassware. Now imagine tasting beer out of that glass. Sorry, we had to break it to you.)

Almost every beer style has its own recommended glass, and thus the bottom line: Use glass. A good, tall Pilsner glass; a tulip; and a tapered pint will take you far. Beer glasses with open mouths, or flared lips, are best for aromatic ales. Online, you can find a wide variety of charts and resources for ordering special glassware at various percentages of your monthly paycheck. If you do want to splurge, look for the ultra-high-quality beer glassware by Spiegelau, especially the stemmed, tulip-shaped glass that has been adopted by some of the best restaurants and beer bars in America. But don't count out your local dollar store. We've found surprisingly attractive stemmed tulip glasses in those humble aisles.

Chapter 1

CRISP & CLEAN

Plenty of the "light" beers you find at the supermarket offer mere refreshment, in the form of bland, international macrobrews. But the promise of better lightweight beers is that they can be much, much more than fizzy yellow water. A well-made beer that is delicate, effervescent, and minimally flavorful in finish does not mean it has nothing to offer. On the contrary, the easy, refreshing flavors of the beers in this category work very well with food, by contrasting and complementing the mild flavors of certain proteins and carbs; cooling fiery spices; accenting the acidity and pop of citrusy flavors; and, more than anything else, resetting and refreshing the palate, with the help of carbonation that cuts fattiness and seems to scrub the taste buds between sips.

What is a "crisp" beer, exactly? Like a good Muscadet, we think a crisp beer is, essentially, a dry beer—lacking in residual sugars, and deftly hopped to leave the drinker's palate coated with resins (from those hops) and intrigued. As long as they're balanced, the snappier flavors imparted by hops in certain beers, such as the recently popularized India pale lager (IPL), can work well with a range of seafood and vegetable dishes, and are perfect with sociable small plates like the following recipes. With their light, bubbly textures and low alcohol content, the beers featured in this chapter are ideal for serving in the early stages of any evening, including a dinner party.

When it comes to "clean," do we mean other beers are "dirty"? Not exactly. Many craft beers are unfiltered and unpasteurized, leaving nutritious yeast in suspension—and therefore not shining with glasslike clarity—but that doesn't keep them from having distinct, elegantly balanced flavors that go beautifully with food. In brewers' parlance, "clean" means a beer brewed perfectly straight, with no (accidental) infections or additions (for style) of "funky" yeasts, fruits, spices, and other such influences.

To the beer consumer, a "clean" beer is also, more often than not, a dry beer, fully attenuated—that is, one that is fermented to total dryness—which simply leaves the palate refreshed and looking for more. A beer can be both clean and dry but unfiltered, as with kellerbier, an unfiltered light lager until recently usually found only in breweries and brewpubs, but now becoming more available. Other notable styles in this chapter include helles, or light lagers from Germany; Czech-style Pilsners; and light-bodied American cream ales. There are also some surprises—did you realize that dry Irish stout, for which beloved slow-pour Guinness is practically eponymous, is very much a light beer? More than anything, the beer styles racked up in this chapter are built for continuous refreshment between bites of the vibrant, internationally inspired dishes, without sacrificing flavor. Time to break out the stash. The party's just getting started.

CZECHS MIX

OKAY, LET'S GET IT STARTED. This Czech-inspired version of a classic American beer-drinking snack uses paprika and dry milk for an extra-savory seasoning that clings to each crunchy nibble. Of all the light, crisp, and clean-tasting beer styles best suited for sipping with the mix, there's one that stands head and shoulders above the rest: Pilsner, or pils. Originating in the verdant rolling hills of Bohemia (the area now anchored by the Czech Republic), Pilsner is a lager beer (meaning it's cleanly cold-fermented and cold-conditioned for four to five weeks), typically 4.5 to 5.5% ABV, pale to straw gold in color, with a pronounced spiciness (derived from noble hops) and a thirst-quenching bite.

Although Czech and German breweries originated the style, American pils brewers have really shone amid the craft-beer renaissance. For example, Pivo Hoppy Pils, by Firestone Walker in Paso Robles, California, would be an ideal match here. Pivo (Czech for "beer") is a 5.3% ABV brew made in the tradition of leaner German Pilsners, but with the additional, American-style oomph of aromatic Saphir hops, redolent of bergamot and lemongrass. Its lacy head, lip-smacking finish, and overall balance pair perfectly with this nutty mix's familiar, savory flavors. If you don't have access to a great local offering (pils is best very fresh), good alternatives are import versions like EKU Pils from Germany's Kulmbacher brewery or, as a fail-safe option, Pilsner Urquell, the oldest commercial version of the style. (If it's been well kept, out of sunlight and held at the right cold temperature, it can be a great beer.) The inexpensive, German-style Bitburger Pils, available at many Trader Joe's stores, is a reliable standby for your pantry, too.

Makes about 8 cups/800 g

- 3 CUPS/185 G WHEAT CHEX CEREAL
- 1 CUP/40 G THIN PRETZEL STICKS
- 1 CUP/145 G UNSALTED ALMONDS
- 1 CUP/130 G UNSALTED CASHEWS
- ⅓ CUP/50 G SUNFLOWER SEEDS
- 3 LARGE GARLIC CLOVES, MINCED
- ¼ CUP/35 G NONFAT DRY MILK POWDER
- 2 TBSP HUNGARIAN PAPRIKA
- 1½ TSP FINE SEA SALT
- 1 TSP ONION POWDER
- ½ CUP/110 G UNSALTED BUTTER
- 2 TBSP WORCESTERSHIRE SAUCE

1. Preheat the oven to 250°F/120°C.

2. Stir together the cereal, pretzel sticks, almonds, cashews, sunflower seeds, and garlic in a large bowl. Stir together the milk powder, paprika, salt, and onion powder in a separate small bowl. Sprinkle the seasoning mixture over the cereal mixture and stir until evenly coated.

3. Put the butter in a large roasting pan and place it in the oven to melt. When the butter is melted, after 2 to 5 minutes, remove the pan from the oven and stir in the Worcestershire sauce. Add the cereal mixture to the pan and stir until evenly coated with the butter mixture. Spread in an even layer.

4. Return the pan to the oven and bake until the mix is dry and crisp, about 1 hour, stirring every 15 minutes or so. Let cool before serving. (Store leftovers in an airtight container at room temperature for up to 1 week.)

OUR RECOMMENDED BREWS:

Pivo Hoppy Pils FIRESTONE WALKER BREWING COMPANY / **Pils** HEATER ALLEN BREWING / **Prima Pils** VICTORY /
EKU Pils KULMBACHER BRAUEREI / **Pilsner Urquell** PLZENSKY PRASDROJ / **Bitburger Pils** BITBURGER BRAUEREI / **Pilsner** BREAKSIDE BREWERY

CHILE AND HONEY POPCORN

KÖLSCH

WHAT COULD BE MORE SOCIAL THAN BEER AND POPCORN?

And to keep the vibe really mellow, any wise popcorn chef will use this genius technique: Heat the kernels slowly, in hot oil but off the stove top, until they are about to burst; *then* return the pot to the heat. A symphony of popping kernels crescendos all at once, and the risk of burning is all but eliminated. For beer-pairing with this spicy and slightly sweet take on ever-popular popcorn, a German (or German-style) Kölsch works perfectly. The reasons are subtler than one might expect. Technically a light ale from the northern German city of Köln (Cologne), Kölsch has a faintly sweet, soft malt character and a finish that is crisp and grassy. When brewed according to tradition, Kölsch exhibits a touch of sweetness from a sulfurlike by-product of its fermentation that tastes of cooked or creamed corn—which, of course, really pops with this crowd-pleasing treat. Ideally, Kölsch is poured into a *stange* ("stick"), a straight-sided, 7-oz/210-ml glass (as mandated by the Kölsch Konvention of 1986—really!), but hey, do what you can.

Look for a Köln brew such as Reissdorf; or, opt for one of the killer Kölsch-style beers emerging from many microbreweries. In summertime, try Alaskan Summer Ale, which is brewed in Juneau using glacier water and exhibits bready flavor and just enough lip-smacking hops. Portland, Oregon's Occidental also has a stellar offering. For something more experimental, try the hops-forward Ottekelong from Freigeist, an unfiltered version of the style.

Serves 6 to 8

3 TBSP PEANUT OIL OR VEGETABLE OIL
½ CUP/110 G POPCORN KERNELS
3 FRESH THYME SPRIGS
¼ CUP/60 ML EXTRA-VIRGIN OLIVE OIL
2 TBSP HONEY
1 TSP FINE SEA SALT
½ TO 1 TSP CHIMAYO OR NEW MEXICO CHILE POWDER

1. Heat the peanut oil in a large, deep pot with a tight-fitting lid over medium-high heat until shimmering. Add 3 popcorn kernels, cover tightly, and listen: When you hear the kernels pop, add the rest of the popcorn, along with the thyme sprigs. Cover and shake to mix it all together, then remove from the heat and count to thirty.

2. Return the pot to medium-high heat and listen for the popcorn to begin popping, which will happen quickly. Once the popping begins, put on oven mitts and gently shake the pot over the burner. Set the lid slightly ajar to allow steam to escape; this will result in crisper popcorn.

3. When the popping slows to just a few pops per second, remove the pot from the heat and keep covered until the popping stops, 20 to 30 seconds longer, shaking often. Pour the popcorn into a large bowl.

4. Wipe out the pot with paper towels to remove any bits of corn or kernel skin, if needed. Combine the olive oil, honey, salt, and chile powder to taste in the warm pot. Stir until the mixture is well blended and warmed through, then drizzle it over the popcorn and toss well to coat evenly. Serve immediately.

OUR RECOMMENDED BREWS:

Kölsch BRAUEREI HEINRICH REISSDORF; OCCIDENTAL BREWING CO. / **Alaskan Summer Ale** ALASKAN BREWING CO. / **Ottekelong** FREIGEIST BIERKULTUR / **Brothers' Gold** KUHNHENN BREWING

KIMCHI QUESADILLAS

AMERICAN PALE LAGER

THE NEXT GENERATION OF AMERICAN BEER FOOD HAS ARRIVED. Inspired by the Kogi Korean BBQ taco truck in L.A., these ultra-savory snacks demand a clean, cooling beer that will stand up to the heat and spice of the kimchi without washing out completely. Since the invention—and global domination—of Pilsner and other pale and golden lagers in the 1840s, the overarching family of pale lagers has become an international standard. But the surprising thing is how many variations within this "international lager" category there are. In the United States, Budweiser (and its even more commercially successful sibling Bud Light) is the popular placeholder for this style of beer, but its watery nature belies an attention to cost-cutting rather than flavor. Instead, seek out a craft-brewed version of the style, such as American Darling by the Pretty Things Beer and Ale Project, out of Boston; Anchor California Lager; or Full Sail Session Lager. Serve very cold, with gusto.

Serves 4 to 6

FOUR 8-IN/20-CM FLOUR TORTILLAS

1½ CUPS/130 G SHREDDED MEXICAN-STYLE FOUR-CHEESE BLEND

2 CUPS/270 G CABBAGE KIMCHI, DRAINED AND CHOPPED

1 TBSP PEANUT OIL OR VEGETABLE OIL

4 GREEN ONIONS, WHITE AND GREEN PARTS, THINLY SLICED

HANDFUL OF FRESH CILANTRO SPRIGS, THIN STEMS AND LEAVES ONLY

1. Place the tortillas on a work surface. Cover half of each tortilla with the cheese and then the kimchi, dividing them evenly. Fold the empty half of each tortilla over the fillings.

2. Heat a 12-in/30.5-cm skillet, preferably cast iron, over medium heat. Add 2 tsp of the peanut oil and swirl to coat the pan. Put two of the quesadillas in the pan and cook, turning once, until the cheese is melted and the tortillas are nicely toasted, 3 to 5 minutes per side. Transfer the cooked quesadillas to a cutting board. Add the remaining 1 tsp oil to the pan and repeat to cook the remaining two quesadillas.

3. Cut the quesadillas into wedges and arrange them on a platter or individual plates. Sprinkle with the green onions, mound the cilantro sprigs in the center, and serve immediately.

OUR RECOMMENDED BREWS:

American Darling PRETTY THINGS BEER AND ALE PROJECT / **California Lager** ANCHOR / **Hoponious Union** JACK'S ABBY / **Session Lager** FULL SAIL / **Joe's Premium American Pilsner** AVERY / **329 Lager** GOLDEN ROAD

LIPTAUER ON RYE
WITH SLICED RADISH

MUNICH HELLES LAGER OR KELLERBIER

THE BEST BEER GARDEN IN MUNICH LIES IN THE VIKTUALIEN-MARKT, A TWO-HUNDRED-YEAR-OLD FARMERS' MARKET IN THE CENTER OF TOWN. Arrayed in its 140 or so stalls are the best produce and artisan foods the area has to offer. And the *markt* has another irresistible tradition: While taking a beer break, visitors love to snack on thinly sliced, salted white radishes on toast with butter and chives. The peppery radish, delicate onions, and rich butter combine to be both thirst-inducing and satisfying without being too filling. In this variation, liptauer—a garlicky, paprika-kissed cheese spread—ups the butter's game.

For your beer choice, nothing makes more sense than a true Munich *helles* ("light") beer, also known as *hell*, with the satisfying dry snap of noble hops and yet enough bready malt flavors to complement the tangy, nutty cheese spread. Or, a terrific unfiltered and unpasteurized helles-style beer you can find in very good beer shops is a light lager called *kellerbier*. The best of its kind we know is a bit of a mouthful: Ungespundet Hefetrüb, from Mahr's Bräu, in Eastern Bavaria. It's cloudy, full-bodied, and flavorful, with a mild, pleasant buttery aroma and richness to spare despite a low alcohol percentage.

Makes 16 to 20 bites

8 OZ/230 G QUARK, FARMER CHEESE, OR COTTAGE CHEESE

½ CUP/110 G UNSALTED BUTTER, AT ROOM TEMPERATURE, CUT INTO CUBES

4 CORNICHONS OR 6 DILL PICKLE SLICES, FINELY CHOPPED, PLUS A LITTLE OF THE JUICE

3 TBSP THINLY SLICED GREEN ONIONS, WHITE AND LIGHT GREEN PARTS ONLY

2½ TBSP CAPERS, DRAINED AND RINSED

½ SMALL GARLIC CLOVE, MASHED TO A PASTE

1 TSP SWEET PAPRIKA

1 TSP DIJON MUSTARD

1 TSP CARAWAY SEEDS, LIGHTLY CRUSHED

FINE SEA SALT AND FRESHLY GROUND PEPPER

1 LOAF DARK RYE BREAD

1 BUNCH RADISHES, TRIMMED AND THINLY SLICED

2 TBSP EXTRA-VIRGIN OLIVE OIL

1. Combine the quark and butter in a stand mixer or a large bowl. Beat together until smooth, using the paddle attachment or a sturdy wooden spoon. Add the cornichons, green onions, capers, garlic, ½ tsp of the paprika, the mustard, and caraway seeds. Season with salt and pepper and mix together well. Taste and adjust the seasoning, adding a little of the pickle juice to brighten the flavors, if needed. Transfer to a small bowl. Cover and refrigerate until chilled, at least 1 hour, but the flavor will continue to develop overnight. (The liptauer can be made up to 3 days in advance.)

2. Cut the bread into canapé-size slices and toast them lightly. When cooled, spread each toast with a thick smear of the liptauer. Fan several slices of radish over the cheese. Whisk together the olive oil and the remaining ½ tsp paprika and drizzle a bit over each canapé just before serving.

OUR RECOMMENDED BREWS:

Lagerbier Hell AUGUSTINER-BRÄU / **Hell** SURLY / **Gold Lager** STOUDT'S / **Crank Tank Lager** SWEETWATER / **Ungespundet-hefetrüb** MAHR'S BRÄU

FRIED PICKLED VEGETABLES
WITH HOMEMADE RANCH DIP

PALE LAGER

LIKE BEER, PICKLES CAN BE MISUNDERSTOOD. The product of careful fermentation, a great pickle is much more than a condiment; these days, it's a conversation—sociable, and engaging. Chances are, you've got more of them around than you thought—pretty gift jars, holiday and farmers' market impulses. Perhaps you've even made them yourself, and those Mason jars in the back of the fridge are getting a bit lonesome. Not to worry, this recipe means new life for any pickled vegetables you have on hand (as long as they are good quality). And this recipe is a great first plate for beer tastings and assorted backyard *bricolage*—that is, tinkering.

In the American South—thanks to a guy we wish we'd met named Bernell "Fatman" Austin, whose Duchess Drive-In, in Atkins, Arkansas, put them on the menu—a properly fried pickle is reason enough to pull over and stay awhile. Generally small in stature, the salty, herbal, pungent, and sour flavors—created through anaerobic fermentation (in brine or vinegar solutions, and thus without oxygen)—are mighty indeed. Luckily, we have beer.

Depending on the power of your pickles, you'll be tempted to pick a beer with firepower to match, but trust us, it's best to keep it simple. Palate-cleansing, super-light American-style lagers will make nice with most pickles, including your half-sours. Pickles with amped-up spice or super-sours may demand something a little more assertive—or just another tall draught of the same. Try Victory Throwback Lager, Yuengling Lager, or New Belgium's Shift, which has a bit of extra tang.

Serves 4 to 6

RANCH DIP

½ CUP/120 ML BUTTERMILK

3 TBSP SOUR CREAM

2 TBSP MAYONNAISE

1 TBSP MINCED FRESH CHIVES

1 TBSP FINELY MINCED FRESH TARRAGON, DILL, AND PARSLEY, OR ANY COMBINATION OF THE THREE

1 LARGE GARLIC CLOVE, MASHED TO A PASTE

½ TSP DIJON MUSTARD

½ TSP RED WINE VINEGAR

FINE SEA SALT AND FRESHLY GROUND PEPPER

FRIED PICKLES

1 CUP/120 G ALL-PURPOSE FLOUR

1 CUP/240 ML BUTTERMILK

1½ CUPS/165 G DRIED BREAD CRUMBS

1 TBSP OLD BAY OR CAJUN SEASONING

½ TSP FINE SEA SALT

12 OZ/340 G DRAINED MIXED PICKLED VEGETABLES SUCH AS DILL-PICKLED CUCUMBER SLICES, GREEN BEANS, FENNEL, SLICED BEETS, CARROT SPEARS, MUSHROOMS, AND CAULIFLOWER

PEANUT OIL OR VEGETABLE OIL FOR FRYING

1. **TO MAKE THE DIP:** Whisk together the buttermilk, sour cream, mayonnaise, chives, mixed herbs, garlic, mustard, and vinegar in a bowl. Season with salt and pepper. Pour the dip into a serving dish, cover, and refrigerate until ready to serve.

2. **TO MAKE THE FRIED PICKLES:** Put the flour in a large bowl and the buttermilk in a second large bowl. In a third large bowl, whisk together the bread crumbs, Old Bay seasoning, and salt. Line the bowls up in that order. Spread the pickled vegetables on paper towels and pat dry.

3. Pour peanut oil into a large pot to a depth of 1 in/2.5 cm. Heat over medium-high heat until it registers 375°F/190°C on a deep-frying thermometer. Meanwhile, line a large baking sheet with paper towels and set it near the stove.

4. One or two at a time, toss the pickled vegetables in the flour until well coated and shake off the excess. Next dip them in the buttermilk, letting the excess drip back into the bowl. Finally, toss them in the bread-crumb mixture, patting on the breading to coat well and help it adhere evenly. Collect the breaded vegetables on a second large baking sheet (unlined) as you work.

5. Lower some of the breaded vegetables into the oil; do not crowd the pot. Fry until golden brown and crunchy, 1 to 2 minutes, adjusting the heat as needed to maintain the temperature of the oil. Remove the fried vegetables with a slotted spoon or skimmer as they are finished and transfer them to the prepared baking sheet to drain. Repeat to fry the remaining vegetables, allowing the oil to return to 375°F/190°C between each batch.

6. When all of the vegetables are fried and drained, transfer them to a platter and serve immediately, with the dip.

OUR RECOMMENDED BREWS:

Throwback Lager VICTORY **/ Yuengling Lager** D. G. YUENGLING & SON **/ Shift Lager** NEW BELGIUM BREWING **/**
1903 Lager CRAFTSMAN BREWING COMPANY **/ The One They Call Zoe** HOPS & GRAIN BREWERY

MAINE LOBSTER ROLLS

CREAM ALE & KÖLSCH

THIS VERSION OF THE CLASSIC NEW ENGLAND LOBSTER ROLL HAS EVERYTHING GOING FOR IT: LUSCIOUS, FRESHLY COOKED LOBSTER; A COOL, CREAMY DRESSING (LIGHT ON THE MAYO AND NOT TOO GLOPPY); THE CRUNCH OF CELERY; AND A LIVELY ZING FROM LEMON AND MINCED CHIVES. In Maine, they've perfected the bun for their famous heavenly hand rolls: a simple hot dog–style bun but without crust on the sides, exposing the bread to spread with butter and griddle in a hot skillet. The resulting mix of fine and dive dining is fun, decadent, and summery, calling out for blue-checked tablecloths and a few cold, light American beers.

We love this dish alongside a cream ale—pale, smooth, and unobtrusive, but with enough sweetness to complement the crustacean. The beer's clean finish refreshes but also accents the butter and toasted flavors of the golden-brown roll. Once a beer style that craft brewers ignored, there are now several excellent brands to look for, from Sixpoint's Sweet Action, brewed in Brooklyn, New York, to Pelican Brewery's Kiwanda Cream Ale, on the left coast.

Kölsch (see page 28) is also a great pairing here. It's not a stretch to call cream ale a sort of American Kölsch. Both are pale gold ales, warm-fermented and then cold-conditioned, resulting in "brite" (brewers' parlance for *clear*) palate-cleansers with smooth, clean esters (aromatic compounds formed during fermentation). Kölsch tends to a more assertive dryness and tangy hop character, which melds nicely with the bright lemon and chives.

A side note to stoke your wanderlust: Should you be fortunate enough to travel to Germany and visit a *Kölsch kneipe,* or corner bar, you'll be served by surly (as per tradition) waiters with doughnut-shaped trays, automatically, until you cry uncle. The only trouble? They don't serve lobster rolls in Köln. This delicate beer doesn't travel especially well, but you may find true Köln Kölsch in fine beer stores; the one from Gaffel Becker is noteworthy. Also sample the excellent American versions, including Widmer's Green & Gold Kölsch, a beer made in honor of Major League Soccer's Portland Timbers, and Schlafly Kölsch, out of St. Louis.

Serves 6

½ LEMON, PLUS 1 TBSP FRESH LEMON JUICE

1 LARGE YELLOW ONION, HALVED

TWO 1½-LB/680-G LIVE MAINE LOBSTERS

¼ CUP/60 ML MAYONNAISE

¼ CUP/40 G FINELY DICED CELERY

2 TBSP MINCED FRESH CHIVES

½ TSP FINE SEA SALT

PINCH OF CAYENNE PEPPER

6 HOT DOG BUNS

4 TBSP/55 G UNSALTED BUTTER, MELTED

1. Bring a very large pot of generously salted water to a boil. Squeeze in the juice from the lemon half. Throw the squeezed half into the pot along with the onion halves. Let the water return to a vigorous boil, then lower in the lobsters, headfirst; make sure they are completely covered by the water. Return to a boil, then set a timer for 12 minutes.

2. When the timer goes off, remove the lobsters from the boiling water using tongs and set aside to cool (don't submerge them in cold water or you'll lose some of the flavor; the residual heat will continue cooking the meat to perfection). When they are cool enough to handle, twist off the claws and tails. Cut the tails in half lengthwise with a heavy knife or cleaver. Dig out the meat and chop it into ½-in/12-mm pieces. Crack open the claws with a lobster cracker or by pounding them lightly with a meat mallet. Dig out the meat, taking care to get into every joint and claw tip, and chop it into ½-in/12-mm pieces.

3. Put the lobster meat in a large bowl and add the mayonnaise, celery, chives, 1 Tbsp lemon juice, salt, and cayenne. Stir gently but thoroughly to combine. Refrigerate the salad until well chilled, at least 1 hour.

4. Heat a large skillet, preferably cast iron, over medium heat. Using a sharp serrated knife, trim away a very thin layer from the top and bottom of each bun, just enough to remove the crust, while taking care to keep the buns connected at the hinge. This will create a nice, flat, crust-free surface on each side to toast. Brush the outer cut sides of each bun with melted butter (stir any remaining melted butter into the lobster salad). Arrange in the skillet and toast until golden brown on both sides, about 1½ minutes per side.

5. Fill the toasted buns with the lobster salad and serve immediately.

OUR RECOMMENDED BREWS:

Kiwanda Cream Ale PELICAN PUB AND BREWERY / Sweet Action SIXPOINT BREWERY / Kölsch GAFFEL BECKER & CO. / Green & Gold Kölsch WIDMER BROTHERS BREWERY / Schlafly Kölsch SCHLAFLY BEER

DUCK CARNITAS NACHOS

IN THIS GAME-CHANGING RENDITION OF A BREWPUB STAPLE, DUCK LEGS, RATHER THAN THE TYPICAL PORK SHOULDER, ARE GIVEN THE CARNITAS TREATMENT. The duck is braised with orange peel in malty Mexican beer (a Vienna Lager style, technically speaking) until tender, then the cooking liquid is reduced until almost nothing is left but the rendered fat used to fry the moist duck meat.

The real art of nachos is in the assembly. We like to put them on a large rimmed baking sheet in two layers so that every single chip gets coated in the toppings. This makes for one wickedly large pile of nachos to share with friends—wow them on game day with this decadent upgrade.

For the beer pairing, Vienna Lager—on the malty end of the light and crisp beer spectrum explored in this chapter—makes a smooth companion for any plate of nachos. Especially, we'd say, ones that feature stewed meat; in the best versions of these beers, bitterness and sweetness are in balance, with delicate hopping levels that are ideal for savory, spicy flavors. An obvious choice is Negra Modelo, but if you can find a craft-brewed (albeit slightly heavier) version of Vienna Lager, such as Samuel Adams Boston Lager or Great Lakes Eliot Ness, go for it. The nachos will abide.

Serves 8 to 12

DUCK CARNITAS

1 DRIED NEW MEXICO CHILE

3 LB/1.4 KG DUCK LEGS, RINSED

2 PIECES FRESH ORANGE PEEL, EACH ABOUT ¾ IN/2 CM WIDE AND 2 IN/5 CM LONG

3 GARLIC CLOVES, CRUSHED

1½ TSP KOSHER OR SEA SALT

ONE 12-OZ/360-ML BOTTLE VIENNA LAGER

1 LB/455 G THICK CORN TORTILLA CHIPS

ONE 15-OZ/425-G CAN BLACK BEANS, DRAINED AND RINSED

1½ LB/680 G SHREDDED MEXICAN-STYLE FOUR-CHEESE BLEND

2 JALAPEÑO CHILES, THINLY SLICED

4 GREEN ONIONS, WHITE AND GREEN PARTS, THINLY SLICED

2 CUPS/60 G LOOSELY PACKED FRESH CILANTRO LEAVES

6 THINLY SLICED RADISHES

SALSA, MEXICAN CREMA OR SOUR CREAM, AND LIME WEDGES FOR SERVING

1. TO MAKE THE DUCK CARNITAS: Heat a small, heavy, dry skillet over medium-high heat. Add the chile and toast, turning occasionally, until puffy and deep brownish-red but not black, 2 to 3 minutes. Stem and halve the chile, discard the seeds, and chop finely. Set aside.

CONTINUED

2. Nestle the duck legs in a heavy pot just large enough to fit them snugly in a single, slightly over-lapping layer. Add the toasted chile, orange peel, garlic, and salt. Pour in the lager, then add enough water to barely cover (it's okay if a few points pro-trude). Bring to a boil over medium-high heat, then turn the heat to medium-low and partially cover the pot. Simmer gently until the meat is tender enough to shred with a fork, about 1½ hours. Transfer the duck legs to a cutting board using tongs.

3. Discard the orange peels from the braising liquid. Raise the heat to high and boil until the liquid is almost completely evaporated and about all that's left is the duck fat, about 10 minutes. (First the bubbles will become large and foamy, and then the foam will begin to subside.)

4. Meanwhile, shred the meat into bite-size chunks and finely chop the skin. Discard any excess fat and the bones.

5. Return the duck meat and skin to the pot and fry over medium heat until the meat is browned and crisp on the outside but still moist and tender inside, about 20 minutes. Stir often, being sure to scrape the bottom of the pot. Drain the meat in a colander (or lift it from the fat with a slotted spoon). (The carnitas can be made up to 1 week in advance and stored in the refrigerator, covered in the fat. When you are ready to assemble the nachos, reheat the meat in a small saucepan, and then drain off the fat.)

6. Preheat the oven to 350°F/180°C. Spread about half of the tortilla chips in an even layer on a large rimmed baking sheet. Top with about half each of the duck, the beans, and the cheese. Repeat to create a second layer. Scatter the jalapeños on top.

7. Bake the nachos until the cheese is melted and just beginning to brown in spots, 15 to 20 minutes. Remove from the oven and top with the green onions, then the cilantro, and then the radishes. Serve immediately with the salsa, crema, and lime wedges on the side.

OUR RECOMMENDED BREWS:

Samuel Adams Boston Lager BOSTON BEER COMPANY / **Negra Modelo** GRUPO MODELO / **Eliot Ness** GREAT LAKES / **Lincoln Park Lager** GOOSE ISLAND / **Special Amber** SPRECHER

GOUGÈRE BEEF SLIDERS

DRY IRISH STOUT

SURE, GOUGÈRES, THE AIRY, BURGUNDIAN CHEESE PUFFS TYPICALLY WASHED DOWN WITH WINE, ARE A TREAT BY THEMSELVES. And sliders may be the ultimate beer snack, whatever their bun. But for this elegant riff, we signed that pillowy puff to jam with a juicy, mini ground-beef patty. The resulting decadent duet is delicious *and* a perfect beer-tasting nosh. And for the brew to go with these special sliders, dry Irish stout—the style that Guinness made into a global powerhouse—is just the ticket.

Wait—a stout can be light, crisp, and clean? *Yes.* A light-bodied beer despite its reputation for caloric heft, every Guinness is a reminder that beer's "heaviness" and its density of color don't always correspond; a 12-oz/360-ml bottle of Guinness draft has only 16 calories more than a can of Bud Light, and fewer than Coors, that old standby "Banquet" beer. Dry Irish stout is palate-cleansing, tasty, not too heavy, not too bitter, not too sweet—an easy match for seared ground beef, conjuring a bit of umami (see page 18). One might step up to an India black ale (a.k.a. Cascadian dark ale) to emphasize bigger hoppy and roasted flavors, but to our way of thinking, a nice, light-bodied, not-too-filling stout does the trick.

Serves 4 to 6

GOUGÈRES

¼ CUP/60 ML MILK, PLUS MORE FOR BRUSHING

¼ CUP/60 ML WATER

3 TBSP UNSALTED BUTTER, CUT INTO CUBES

¼ TSP FINE SEA SALT

PINCH OF FRESHLY GROUND PEPPER

½ CUP/60 G ALL-PURPOSE FLOUR

2 LARGE EGGS, AT ROOM TEMPERATURE

3 OZ/85 G GRUYÈRE CHEESE, SHREDDED

PICKLED SHALLOTS

2 LARGE SHALLOTS, THINLY SLICED

¾ CUP/180 ML RED WINE VINEGAR

1 TSP SUGAR

½ TSP FINE SEA SALT

MINI BEEF PATTIES

1½ LB/680 G GROUND BEEF

2 TSP FINE SEA SALT

1 TSP FRESHLY GROUND PEPPER

DASH OF WORCESTERSHIRE SAUCE

2 TBSP PEANUT OIL OR VEGETABLE OIL

DIJON MUSTARD, FINELY SHREDDED ICEBERG LETTUCE, AND MAYONNAISE FOR SERVING

CONTINUED

1. **TO MAKE THE GOUGÈRES:** Position racks in the upper and lower thirds of the oven and preheat to 400°F/200°C. Lightly butter two rimmed baking sheets.

2. Combine the milk, water, butter, salt, and pepper in a medium saucepan and bring to a boil over medium-high heat. Remove the pan from the heat and stir in the flour using a wooden spoon. Return the pan to the stove top and turn the heat to medium. Beat the dough vigorously with the spoon until it is smooth and glossy and pulls away from the sides of the pan, about 1 minute. Remove the pan from the heat and beat in one of the eggs. When the first egg is completely incorporated, add the second egg, along with about half of the cheese. Stir vigorously to combine.

3. Drop tablespoonfuls of the dough onto the pre-pared baking sheets, spacing them at least 1½ in/4 cm apart; you should have about 12 mounds. Brush the tops lightly with milk and sprinkle with the remaining cheese. Bake until puffy and golden brown, about 25 minutes, rotating the pans top to bottom and front to back in the oven halfway through.

4. **TO MAKE THE PICKLED SHALLOTS:** Put the shal-lots in a small bowl. Add the vinegar, sugar, and salt and stir to mix well. Set aside at room temperature to marinate until pickled, about 30 minutes.

5. **TO MAKE THE BEEF PATTIES:** Combine the beef, salt, pepper, and Worcestershire sauce in a large bowl and stir gently to combine; do not overmix. Form the mixture into 12 small patties, again being careful not to handle too much. Heat the peanut oil in a large skillet, preferably cast iron, just until it begins to smoke. Add half of the burger patties and cook, turning once, until browned and crusty on both sides, about 2 minutes per side. Transfer to a plate lined with paper towels to drain. Repeat to fry the remaining patties.

6. Cut the gougères in half horizontally and spread the bottoms with mustard. Position the burger patties over the mustard and top each with a big pinch of lettuce and some pickled shallots. Spread the top halves lightly with mayonnaise and place over the sliders. Serve immediately.

FIERY LAMB SATAY
WITH COOLING CUCUMBER RELISH

INDIA PALE LAGER

BY NOW THE LORE ABOUT INDIA PALE ALES—BORN AMID COLONIAL ENGLAND'S OVERSEAS CAMPAIGNS ON THE INDIAN SUBCONTINENT AND ELSEWHERE, THESE WERE STRONGER AND HIGHLY HOPPED BREWS, TO AVOID SPOILAGE—IS FAMILIAR, IF LIKELY OVERBLOWN. Foot soldiers and mariners were probably drinking less expensive, malty mild ale and porter, while administrators and expat upper-crusters sipped the hoppier, stronger stuff. But no matter. India pale ale is back with a vengeance. Once an oddity, the citrusy, herbaceous tang has created a cottage industry worldwide, with many breweries' flagship ending in the initials "IPA."

It was only a matter of time before the "India-fication" of other styles set in, even outside the ale family, as a sort of catch-all class for beers that are aggressively hopped. This is the nature of craft beer—experimentation is the norm; styles morph and change; tradition is, at times, merely a springboard for flights of fancy. White, black, and other variations of IPA abound these days, with style distinctions beyond hue that eventually become more substantial and codified.

These beers can be tricky to pair with, precisely because that herbal bitterness—while delicious in gin, citrus juice, certain teas, and other foods and drinks—can wreak havoc on foods. But not always. India pale lagers balance the ample, clean, bready flavors of traditional pale lagers with the crisp, flowery, citrus-smack of tangy IPAs, resulting in interesting, quaffable brews that go well with spicy, savory fare, like this satay.

Serves 4 to 6

LAMB SATAY

3 TBSP SEEDLESS TAMARIND PULP (SEE NOTE)

2 TSP CORIANDER SEEDS

1 TSP CUMIN SEEDS

½ TSP PEPPERCORNS

⅔ CUP/160 ML COCONUT MILK (NOT LOW-FAT)

6 GARLIC CLOVES, SMASHED AND PEELED

ONE 2-IN/5-CM PIECE FRESH GINGER, PEELED AND THINLY SLICED

2 OR 3 FRESH RED OR GREEN THAI CHILES, STEMMED

2 TBSP SUGAR

1 TBSP FINE SEA SALT

2 LB/910 G BONELESS LAMB SHOULDER, EXCESS FAT TRIMMED

CUCUMBER RELISH

1 SMALL CUCUMBER

1 LARGE SHALLOT, HALVED LENGTHWISE AND THINLY SLICED CROSSWISE

2 TO 4 RED THAI CHILES, THINLY SLICED

¼ CUP PLUS 2 TBSP/90 ML RICE VINEGAR

¼ CUP/50 G SUGAR

½ TSP FINE SEA SALT

¼ CUP/30 G FINELY CHOPPED PEANUTS

FRESH CILANTRO SPRIGS, THIN STEMS AND LEAVES ONLY, FOR GARNISH

1. TO MAKE THE LAMB SATAY: Combine the tamarind pulp and ⅓ cup/80 ml water in a small saucepan and bring to a boil. Remove from the heat and break up the pulp with a wooden spoon, then cover and set aside to soften, about 10 minutes. Mash up the softened tamarind pulp to dissolve. Pour the mixture through a fine-mesh sieve into a blender, using the back of the wooden spoon to aggressively mash and push as much of the pulp through as possible. Discard the solids.

2. Heat a small, heavy, dry skillet over medium-high heat. Add the coriander seeds, cumin seeds, and peppercorns and toast, swirling the pan constantly, until the seeds are fragrant and lightly browned, about 1 minute. Add the seeds to the blender along with the coconut milk, garlic, ginger, chiles, sugar, and salt and blend to a smooth purée for the marinade.

3. Cut the lamb into pieces about 1½-in/4-cm long, 1-in/2.5-cm wide, and ½-in/12-mm thick. Thread the lamb pieces lengthwise onto wooden skewers, leaving about one-third of each skewer free to use as a handle. (Don't leave gaps between the meat pieces, but don't smush them together too tightly, either, or the lamb won't cook evenly.) Arrange the assembled skewers in a shallow baking dish in a single layer and pour the marinade over, turning the skewers and rubbing the marinade into the meat as needed to coat the lamb evenly. Cover and let marinate in the refrigerator for at least 2 hours or preferably overnight.

4. TO MAKE THE CUCUMBER RELISH: Cut the cucumber in half lengthwise and scoop out the seeds, then cut each half lengthwise into quarters, so you have long wedges (like skinny pickle spears). Thinly slice the wedges crosswise into small triangles. Combine the cucumbers with the shallot, chiles, vinegar, sugar, and salt in a small bowl. Cover and refrigerate for at least 1 hour, or up to 1 day, before serving. (Note, the cucumbers will soften a bit if left to marinate for more than a few hours, but are still delicious.)

5. Prepare a hot fire in a charcoal grill or preheat a gas grill to high. Lightly oil the grill grate. Remove the lamb skewers from the marinade, gently shaking off the excess, and arrange them on the hottest part of the grill. Grill, turning once, until nicely charred on the outside but still slightly pink in the center, 3 to 4 minutes per side for medium. (Because of the cut of meat, rare or medium-rare will be too chewy in this preparation.) Transfer to a serving platter and sprinkle with the peanuts. Scatter the cilantro sprigs over the top and serve hot or at room temperature with the cucumber relish on the side.

NOTE: *Look for seedless tamarind pulp removed from the pod and compressed into a sticky, dense block in Asian markets or grocery stores with a good selection of international foods.*

OUR RECOMMENDED BREWS:

American Dream MIKKELLER **/ Double Agent IPL** SAMUEL ADAMS **/ Speakeasy Metropolis** SPEAKEASY ALES & LAGERS **/ Hopside Down** WIDMER BROTHERS BREWERY **/ Silver & Gold IPL** GREAT LAKES BREWING COMPANY

Chapter 2

FRUIT & SPICE

Doesn't that sound nice?

It's well known that our sense of taste derives almost entirely from our sense of smell. This is a very good reason to make sure you're always drinking in the aromas of your beer with every sip, searching for new dimensions. Plunge your nose into the glass and take a good whiff once in a while; you'll find something new each time.

When it comes to fragrance in beer, fruitiness is largely a by-product of aromatic alcoholic compounds called esters, formed during warm fermentations—in other words, mostly ales, such as the many witbiers in this chapter. One of these powerful metabolite esters, Isoamyl acetate, gives the distinctive flavor to traditional German weisse, and can be tasted in concentrations as low as two parts per million. It's been compared to banana; other esters taste of peach, apricot, kiwi, pear, plum, and various tropical fruits and red berries. Less than desirable esters taste of nail polish remover and green apple. But make no mistake: fruitiness in a beer can be one of its best aspects, enhancing every swallow, especially with the right dish served alongside.

The same yeast helping crank out esters is also playing a role in the production of phenols—flavors found in all beers, as tannins are found in wines. Perhaps the best known (among beer makers, anyway) is 4-vinyl guaiacol, which tastes and smells strongly of clove, another defining trait of German weisse. Belgian yeast strains, used in many of the witbiers in this chapter (and the saisons in chapter 4), tend to impart peppery, spicy notes that contrast pleasingly with any sweetness in the beer, as well as that of whatever dish they're paired with. This is exactly why those beer styles make such good companions to certain foods.

Of course, there's a long (particularly Belgian) tradition of adding actual spices, such as coriander, cumin, Curaçao orange, anise, ginger, and cardamom, among others, to beer. We found that witbier, typically spiced with coriander and Curaçao orange, is a great pairing beer for a wide variety of foods, especially things that are sweet and acidic at the same time, like the tomatoes featured in our playful Fried Burrata Sandwiches with Blood Orange–Tomato Soup (page 50).

This chapter comprises many dishes with long cultural histories, much like the beers they are paired with. The classic quotidian fare—ranging from pepper jelly, cheese, and eggs to cured pork and smoked fish—complements, shows off, and enhances the flavors found in a range of fruity, spicy beer styles.

GRATINÉED BELGIAN ENDIVE
WITH GRUYÈRE

WITBIER

WITBIER IS A GREAT BEER STYLE THAT ALMOST WASN'T: A FOUR-HUNDRED-YEAR-OLD BELGIAN RECIPE, THE PALE, HAZY GOLD BREW, OFTEN SPICED (WITH CORIANDER AND ORANGE PEEL, FOR STARTERS), WOULD LIKELY HAVE COMPLETELY VANISHED, WERE IT NOT FOR THE EFFORTS OF BELGIAN PIERRE CELIS IN THE 1960S. The last brewery making witbier in Belgium closed in 1955, but Celis, then a milkman, launched Hoegaarden Brewery in 1966 to bring back the style—a story that's a saga unto itself. (Due to a fire and various financial difficulties, he wasn't able to hold on to the juggernaut, but he's still credited with reviving the style worldwide, especially through Celis, his Austin, Texas brewery, since closed.)

With a honey sweetness, orangey light tartness, and dry finish, Belgian witbier—such as the organic Foret Blanche, which has something of a musty basement aroma but a clean, fresh finish—is an elegant companion to many foods, especially those exhibiting bright fruity notes.

In this Old World winter dish, the brightness of the witbier complements the savory melted cheese, and the light bitterness of the hops picks up the nuttiness of the cheese.

Serves 6

6 BELGIAN ENDIVES
¼ CUP/60 ML HEAVY CREAM
1 TSP DIJON MUSTARD
½ TSP FINE SEA SALT
3 OZ/85 G THINLY SLICED HAM (OPTIONAL)
4 OZ/115 G GRUYÈRE CHEESE, SHREDDED
BAGUETTE, CUT ON THE DIAGONAL INTO LARGE SLICES AND TOASTED, FOR SERVING

1. Preheat the oven to 400°F/200°C. Butter the bottom of a baking dish.

2. Trim away any browned or blemished parts of the endives and the tough tips of the root ends. Cut them in half lengthwise, but keep the root ends intact.

3. Arrange the endives in a single layer in the prepared dish, cut-side down. Mix together the cream, mustard, and salt in a bowl. Drizzle the cream mixture over the endives. Cover the dish tightly with aluminum foil and bake until the endives are tender when pierced with a fork, 25 to 30 minutes.

4. Remove the endives from the oven and preheat the broiler. Tear the ham slices (if using) into pieces roughly the size of the endive halves and drape a piece over each half. Sprinkle the cheese over the top. Broil until the cheese is melted and lightly browned in spots, 3 to 4 minutes. Remove from the broiler and let cool for 5 minutes.

5. Place each endive half on top of a toasted baguette slice, and divide them among six plates. (Save any extra toasts for mopping up the leftover pan juices.) Spoon some of the pan juices over each to saturate the bread. Serve immediately.

OUR RECOMMENDED BREWS:
Foret Blanche BRASSERIE DUPONT / **Blanche de Brooklyn** BROOKLYN BREWERY / **Orchard White** THE BRUERY / **La Perouse** MAUI BREWING CO. / **White Rascal** AVERY

SWEET CORN GRIDDLE CAKES

HEFEWEIZEN

THE SWEETNESS OF CORN IS THE SWEETNESS OF LATE SUMMER, WHEN THE GARDEN IS IN FULL BLOOM AND THE BEST DAYS ARE SPENT OUTSIDE, EATING AND DRINKING WITH FRIENDS. Now, while that may be an ideal scenario for this ultimately comforting appetizer, it's delicious year-round—transcendent with kernels cut straight off a fresh cob, but still top-notch with good-quality frozen corn.

Beer lovers will do well to take a cue from the Bavarians, who enjoy a bit of weissbier in the A.M. (there's no harm, in moderation) and tuck into these sweet-and-savory cakes for brunch, paired with a spritzy, traditional German hefeweizen such as caramel-hued Schneider—faintly sweet and spicy, perfectly palate-cleansing.

Hefeweizen (meaning "yeast-wheat"), a cloudy wheat-based ale, was one of the first German styles to become popular in the American craft-brewing scene in the 1980s and 1990s, led by Widmer's effervescent, easy-drinking version, which was usually served with a lemon. Though Germans wouldn't dare (or deign to) add the garnish, the Portland-brewed beer helped propel Widmer to stardom—and inspired many an excellent craft brew along similar lines.

The griddle cakes' brown-butter flavors work with the beer's caramelized wheat malts and, in traditional German versions, touch of spice (particularly clove). The griddle cakes are delicious on their own, but can be topped with a thin slice of smoked salmon or a small pinch of salmon roe to enhance the savoriness, if you like.

Serves 4

1½ CUPS/300 G FRESH YELLOW SWEET CORN KERNELS OR THAWED FROZEN CORN

¼ CUP/40 G CORNMEAL, GRITS, OR POLENTA

¼ CUP/30 G ALL-PURPOSE FLOUR

¼ CUP/30 G FRESHLY GRATED PARMIGIANO-REGGIANO CHEESE

1 LARGE EGG, BEATEN

3 TBSP MINCED FRESH CHIVES

1 TBSP SOUR CREAM, PLUS MORE FOR GARNISH

1 TSP FINE SEA SALT

¼ TSP FRESHLY GROUND PEPPER

2 TBSP UNSALTED BUTTER, PLUS MORE AS NEEDED

2 TBSP OLIVE OIL, PLUS MORE AS NEEDED

1. Preheat the oven to 200°F/95°C.

2. Combine the corn, cornmeal, flour, cheese, egg, 1½ Tbsp of the chives, the sour cream, salt, and pepper in a medium bowl and stir thoroughly to make a thick batter. Cover and let rest for at least 30 minutes, or refrigerate up to 12 hours.

3. Heat a large cast-iron skillet or sauté pan over medium heat. Add the butter and olive oil. When the foam has subsided, drop four dollops of batter, about 2 Tbsp each, in the hot pan. Flatten the dollops with a spatula. When the cakes are browned and crisp on the bottom, after about 3 minutes, carefully flip them and cook until browned on the second side, about 3 minutes longer. Transfer the cakes to a platter and keep warm in the oven. Repeat with the remaining batter, adding more butter and/or olive oil to the pan, if needed.

4. Serve the griddle cakes hot, topped with sour cream and the remaining chives.

OUR RECOMMENDED BREWS:

Weisse Original SCHNEIDER / **Bräu-Weisse** AYINGER / **Hefe Weissebier** WEIHENSTEPHANER / **Hefeweizen** WIDMER / **Hefe Weizen** LIVE OAK / **Kellerweis** SIERRA NEVADA

BLUE CHEESE BISCUITS
WITH COUNTRY HAM AND PEPPER JELLY

WITBIER

WITH THESE BISCUITS, WE'RE NOT GOING FOR FLAKY AND SOFT, WE'RE GOING FOR CRUNCHY ON THE OUTSIDE WITH TENDER, CRUMBLY, BUTTERY, CHEESY BITS INSIDE. The blue cheese in this mix is redolent in a way that's present but far from overpowering, especially in combination with good country ham and piquant pepper jelly.

These biscuits are a welcome accompaniment to almost any meal, but we particularly love to show them off at the brunch table. And what's the best beer to drink with brunch? A coriander-and-orange-smacked witbier is fun, easy, refreshing, and, well, brunchy, because of the bright fruit and spice. Ideally you would procure a barrel-aged version, such as Nomader Wit from Evil Twin, based in Denmark, in which contact with wood deepens flavors considerably. With this dish, the character of the yeast in the Nomader Wit (*Brettanomyces*) accented all of the flavors—ham, buttermilk, blue cheese, and sweet hot-pepper jelly—across the board.

Makes 12 biscuits

2¼ CUPS/270 G ALL-PURPOSE FLOUR

2 TSP BAKING POWDER

1 TSP SUGAR

½ TSP BAKING SODA

½ TSP FINE SEA SALT

5 OZ/140 G COLD BLUE CHEESE, CUT INTO CUBES OR CRUMBLED

½ CUP/110 G COLD UNSALTED BUTTER, CUT INTO CUBES

1 CUP/240 ML COLD, WELL-SHAKEN BUTTERMILK

HEAVY CREAM FOR BRUSHING

GOOD-QUALITY PEPPER JELLY (HOT OR MILD, RED OR GREEN) FOR SPREADING

12 THIN SLICES COUNTRY HAM

1. Preheat the oven to 400°F/200°C. Line a rimmed baking sheet with parchment paper.

2. Mix together the flour, baking powder, sugar, baking soda, and salt in a large bowl or food processor. Add the blue cheese and butter and cut them into the flour mixture using a pastry cutter, or by pulsing the food processor, until the mixture is clumped into bits about the size of peas.

3. Dump the mixture into a large bowl if you used a food processor. Pour the buttermilk over the top and toss gently with a fork until moist clumps form. Turn the dough out onto a lightly floured work surface and gather it together, gently patting and pressing it into a rectangle about 1 in/2.5 cm thick. Be careful not to overwork the dough or the biscuits will be tough; it should still be clumpy and just barely hold together. Press against the edges with a ruler or bench scraper to square off the corners. Cut the rectangle into 12 squares, dipping the knife in flour between cuts to prevent sticking.

4. Arrange the biscuits on the prepared baking sheet, spacing them generously, and brush the tops lightly with cream. Bake until the edges and bottoms are golden brown, about 25 minutes. Let the biscuits cool for at least 10 minutes.

5. Cut the biscuits in half horizontally and spread the cut sides of the bottoms with a dab of pepper jelly, then fold a piece of ham on each and replace the tops. Serve warm or at room temperature.

OUR RECOMMENDED BREWS:

Nomader Wit EVIL TWIN / **White** ALLAGASH / **St. Bretta** CROOKED STAVE / **Blanche** FANTÔME / **Double White** SOUTHAMPTON

FRIED BURRATA SANDWICHES
WITH BLOOD ORANGE–TOMATO SOUP

WITBIER

PERHAPS THIS CLASSIC SNACK FROM NAPLES IS THE ORIGINAL FRIED MOZZARELLA STICK. Mozzarella *in carozza*, or "in a carriage," is an Italian antipasto of fresh mozzarella sandwiched between two slices of white bread, then breaded and fried. But when made with the fresh, cream-filled mozzarella balls called *burrata*, the sandwiches are rich, crispy, and ethereal, bearing little resemblance to anything from a box in the freezer aisle.

Perhaps surprisingly, Italian cuisine presents a variety of challenges for beer pairings. The simultaneous sweetness and acidity of tomato-based sauces, for example, can clash with beer, even as herbs, creamy cheese, fried elements, bready crusts, and citrus notes set up complementary flavors. So what to pick? Mass-produced beers such as Peroni, Moretti, and Poretti are no help; they're seldom better than mass-produced American lagers—sometimes improbably worse—and are often packaged in skunk-prone green glass. A fresh keg on draft at the pool hall? Sure, why not. But in general, these are best avoided.

Don't get us wrong. While it might seem that aside from pizza, beer and Italian fare were simply not meant to walk down the Via dell'Amore, something remarkable happened in Italy over the past twenty years or so: craft brewing has found a new home. Baladin brewery, established in 1996 in Piozzo (Piedmont), ushered in a nationwide fascination with craft beers that has grown and grown. The range of beers created in the *bel paese* is now vast, with some four hundred breweries in operation. Spice tends to lead the flavor profiles, and complex sour beers are popping up all over. (Try the Super Baladin, paired with our buttermilk fried oysters on page 134.)

All that said, for this luxurious lunchtime dish, we recommend another beer, a nice, fresh witbier, the pale, fruity, coriander-and-orange-kissed ale of Belgium. It's light and citrusy enough not to overpower the delicate burrata, but has a spicy kick from coriander seed that works amazingly well with the orange-spiked, slightly sweet soup.

Serves 4 to 6

BLOOD ORANGE–TOMATO SOUP

4 TBSP/55 G UNSALTED BUTTER

½ MEDIUM SWEET ONION, CHOPPED

4 GARLIC CLOVES, CHOPPED

ONE 28-OZ/794-G CAN ITALIAN PLUM TOMATOES, WITH JUICE, FINELY CHOPPED

1½ TSP FINE SEA SALT

6 TO 8 FRESH BASIL LEAVES

JUICE OF 1 BLOOD ORANGE AND 1 TSP FINELY GRATED BLOOD ORANGE ZEST

FRIED BURRATA SANDWICHES

12 SLICES WHITE ITALIAN BREAD

KOSHER OR SEA SALT

1 CUP/120 G ALL-PURPOSE FLOUR

4 LARGE EGGS

3 BALLS FRESH BURRATA, ABOUT 8 OZ/230 G TOTAL, DRAINED

OLIVE OIL AND PEANUT, VEGETABLE, OR OTHER NEUTRAL OIL FOR FRYING

1. **TO MAKE THE SOUP:** Melt the butter in a pot over medium-high heat. Add the onion and cook until softened and just beginning to brown, about 5 minutes. Stir in the garlic and cook until fragrant, about 1 minute longer. Add the tomatoes and their juice, 1 cup/240 ml water, the salt, and basil and bring to a boil. Turn the heat to medium-low and cook, stirring occasionally, until the flavors meld and the soup thickens slightly, 20 to 25 minutes. Remove from the heat and let cool a bit.

2. Working in two batches, process the soup in a blender or food processor until very smooth, about 2 minutes per batch. Return the soup to the pot, add the orange juice and zest, and bring to a gentle simmer over medium-low heat, just to warm through. Taste and adjust the seasoning, and add a little more water if it seems too thick. (The soup will keep, tightly covered in the refrigerator, for up to 4 days. Reheat gently over low heat to serve.)

3. **TO MAKE THE SANDWICHES:** Preheat the oven to 300°F/150°C. Place a wire cooling rack over a large rimmed baking sheet.

4. Trim the crusts from the bread. Set the bread aside and spread the crusts on a second rimmed baking sheet. Bake until fully dried, 15 to 20 minutes. Let cool to room temperature, then process in a food processor to fine crumbs.

5. Sift the dried bread crumbs through a medium-mesh sieve into a large, shallow bowl. (Discard the larger pieces left in the sieve, or reserve for another use.) Season the bread crumbs with a big pinch of salt. Put the flour in another large, shallow bowl. Beat the eggs with a big pinch of salt in a third bowl. Arrange the bowls on a countertop in the following order: flour, eggs, bread crumbs.

6. Cut the bread slices in half diagonally. Cut each ball of burrata into quarters, making sure that each piece has an even portion of the creamy filling. Place a burrata chunk on 12 pieces of the bread, taking care that no cheese protrudes over the edges. Cover each with the remaining 12 pieces of bread and press gently to help them hold together.

7. Begin breading the sandwiches one at a time. First, coat the edges only in the flour; then dip the entire sandwich in the egg; then dip the entire sandwich in the bread crumbs, patting to help the crumbs adhere for an even coating. Arrange the coated sandwiches on the prepared rack as you work.

8. Pour a mixture of half olive oil and half peanut oil into a large skillet to a depth of ¾ in/2 cm and heat over medium-high heat. When the oil reaches 325°F/165°C, or when a crumb of bread sizzles enthusiastically, gently add some of the sandwiches, being careful not to overcrowd the pan. Fry until golden on both sides, turning once, about 2 minutes per side. Transfer the fried sandwiches back to the rack or to paper towels to drain. Repeat to fry the rest of the sandwiches. Adjust the heat as needed to maintain the oil temperature, and be sure to allow the oil to return to 325°F/165°C between batches

9. Serve the sandwiches piping hot, with small cups of the soup for dipping.

SEAFOOD CEVICHE
WITH CRUNCHY QUINOA

BERLINER WEISSE

CEVICHE, A SOUTH AMERICAN SPECIALTY DISH OF COLD MARINATED FISH, IS ALL ABOUT FRESHNESS—OF THE FISH (REPEAT AFTER US: THOU SHALL NOT SKIMP!); OF THE BRIGHT, CITRUS FLAVORS; AND OF THE FESTIVE PRESENTATION. Popular in Peru, Ecuador, and Colombia (where craft brewing has recently taken hold), ceviche's definitive origins are shrouded in mystery. One theory holds that ancient Incans ate a similar dish of fish marinated in *chicha*, a fermented Andean beverage made of corn and manioc. Variations abound, but they are all based on raw seafood and citrus juice (primarily lemon or lime), which slowly "cooks" the food with its acidity. The toasted quinoa in this version adds enlivening texture to contrast the tender fish.

There are several prevailing notions about pairing beer with ceviche. We feel that Pilsner, while often recommended, can clash, due to its assertive, bittering hops. Instead, we found that matching acid with acid, by pouring a light-bodied Berliner weisse, the tart but clean-finishing German sour, set off the tropical flavors in this dish beautifully. Gose, a sour, wheat-based salt-and-coriander-spiced beer, blends very well, too. The salt sets off the citrus notes, like a margarita. *Salud!*

Serves 6 to 8

¼ CUP/45 G RED QUINOA, RINSED AND DRAINED

FINE SEA SALT AND FRESHLY GROUND PEPPER

8 OZ/230 G SASHIMI-GRADE SKINLESS MEATY OCEAN FISH SUCH AS SNAPPER, HALIBUT, OR SEA BASS, CUT INTO ½-IN/12-MM CUBES

4 OZ/115 G SEA SCALLOPS (3 OR 4), CUT INTO ½-IN/12-MM PIECES, OR BAY SCALLOPS

4 OZ/115 G MEDIUM SHRIMP (10 TO 12), PEELED, DEVEINED, AND CUT INTO ½-IN/12-MM PIECES

½ SMALL RED ONION, THINLY SLICED

½ CUP/120 ML FRESH LEMON JUICE

½ CUP/120 ML FRESH LIME JUICE

½ CUP/120 ML FRESH ORANGE JUICE

¼ CUP/7 G FINELY CHOPPED FRESH CILANTRO

2 TBSP EXTRA-VIRGIN OLIVE OIL

1 TSP SUGAR

1 RIPE MANGO, PITTED, PEELED, AND FINELY DICED

1 RIPE AVOCADO, PITTED, PEELED, AND FINELY DICED

TORTILLA CHIPS OR SMALL TOSTADAS FOR SERVING

1. Combine the quinoa and a big pinch of salt in a medium saucepan. Add enough water to cover the quinoa by about 1 in/2.5 cm and bring to a boil over high heat. Turn down the heat to maintain a gentle simmer, cover, and cook, stirring occasionally, until the quinoa is tender and the water is absorbed, 15 to 20 minutes. Meanwhile, preheat the oven to 375°F/190°C.

2. Spread the cooked quinoa in an even layer on a large rimmed baking sheet, breaking up any clumps. Bake, gently tossing once or twice with a spatula, until the quinoa is dry and crunchy, 15 to 25 minutes. Let cool completely before using. (The crunchy quinoa can be stored in an airtight container in the refrigerator for up to 1 week.)

3. Combine the fish, scallops, shrimp, and onion in a medium nonreactive bowl. Add the lemon juice, lime juice, and orange juice and fold gently to combine. Poke any exposed pieces under the liquid as needed so the seafood is all completely submerged. Cover the bowl and refrigerate until the fish is "cooked" to medium-rare by the acid of the citrus juices, 30 to 45 minutes, or up to 4 hours if you prefer it fully cooked. Stir occasionally so the seafood marinates evenly.

4. Drain the ceviche in a colander, discarding the juice. Put the ceviche back in the bowl and toss with the cilantro, olive oil, and sugar. Season with salt and pepper. Refrigerate until ready to serve, preferably not longer than 2 hours.

5. Gently toss in the mango and avocado just before serving. Mound the ceviche in a large, shallow serving bowl and sprinkle with the crunchy quinoa (reserve any extra for another use). Serve immediately with the tortilla chips for scooping.

OUR RECOMMENDED BREWS:

Star of the North AUGUST SCHELL / Everweisse NIGHTSHIFT / Gose WESTBROOK / Geisterzug Gose FREIGEST BIERKULTUR / Original Ritterguts Gose BRAUHAUS HARTMANNSDORF

SMOKED TROUT BOARD
WITH PICKLED RED CABBAGE, CRÈME FRAÎCHE, AND RYE CRISPS

RYE BEER

SERVED ON A WOODEN CUTTING BOARD AND HIGH-LIGHTED BY THE BRILLIANT FUCHSIA-COLORED CABBAGE, THIS SNACK BOARD MAKES A VISUALLY STRIKING PARTY-STARTER. The assemblage shines with Scandinavian flavors: caraway-and-honey crackers, pickled cabbage, fresh dill, and smoked fish.

To accentuate those flavors and textures, seek out a rye beer—a genre that's not nearly as popular as it could be, partly because brewers seldom use much rye. As it turns out, malted rye has no husk, and a lot of protein, which can lead to sticky, messy slowdowns in the brewing process. You needn't worry. The best brewers have it down pat, carrying on the ancient Bavarian, Russian, and Finnish traditions of throwing those distinctive rye malts in the mash tun. The result? Added complexity, mouthfeel, and, for lack of a better word, mojo. "As in bread, or some North American whiskeys, rye adds a grainy, bittersweet, subtle spiciness to beer," wrote the late beer writer Michael Jackson in his classic book *Ultimate Beer*. Anyone else getting thirsty?

Founders' Red's Rye IPA, one of the very best, is brewed with four varieties of Belgian caramel malts and lush Amarillo hops, and shines with a coppery hue. With a clean, grainy malt backbone, the rye and hops in this beer give it an appetizing kick.

Serves 4 to 6

PICKLED RED CABBAGE

1 LB/455 G RED CABBAGE, CORED AND VERY FINELY SHREDDED

1 SMALL RED ONION, HALVED AND THINLY SLICED

¼ CUP/40 G KOSHER OR SEA SALT

2 CUPS/480 ML APPLE CIDER VINEGAR

1 CUP/240 ML LAGER

1 TBSP CARAWAY SEEDS

2 TSP PEPPERCORNS

2 BAY LEAVES

½ CUP/100 G SUGAR

2 TSP YELLOW MUSTARD SEEDS

RYE CRISPS

1 CUP/130 G UNBLEACHED ALL-PURPOSE FLOUR

1 CUP/140 G DARK RYE FLOUR

2 TSP CARAWAY SEEDS

1 TSP FINE SEA SALT

¼ CUP/60 ML EXTRA-VIRGIN OLIVE OIL

2 TBSP HONEY

3 TO 4 TBSP LAGER

ONE 8-OZ/225-G SMOKED TROUT FILLET, AT ROOM TEMPERATURE

1 TBSP COARSELY CHOPPED FRESH DILL

½ CUP/120 ML CRÈME FRAÎCHE OR SOUR CREAM

CONTINUED

1. TO MAKE THE PICKLED CABBAGE: Toss the cabbage and red onion with the salt in a large colander and set it in the sink to wilt and drain, about 2 hours. Rinse away the salt and drain well, then dry in a salad spinner or with a clean kitchen towel.

2. Combine the vinegar, lager, caraway seeds, peppercorns, and bay leaves in a sauté pan and bring to a boil over high heat. Continue boiling, stirring occasionally, until the liquid has reduced by half, about 10 minutes. Remove from the heat and stir in the sugar until dissolved.

3. Put the cabbage mixture and mustard seeds in a large bowl. Pour the pickling brine through a fine-mesh sieve into the bowl and stir it all together. Let cool to room temperature. You should have about 4 cups/680 g, so you can re-create the board a few times. (The pickled cabbage is ready to eat right away, or pack it into a large glass jar, pour in the brine, and store in the refrigerator for up to 1 month.)

4. TO MAKE THE CRISPS: Preheat the oven to 375°F/190°C. Lightly grease a large baking sheet.

5. Whisk together the all-purpose flour, rye flour, caraway seeds, and salt in a large bowl. Stir in the olive oil and honey with a fork until evenly dispersed. Slowly drizzle in the lager, while stirring, just until the mixture forms moist clumps. Turn the dough out onto a lightly floured work surface and knead about five times, just to shape it into a smooth disk. Wrap the dough disk in plastic wrap and let rest at room temperature for 10 minutes.

6. Cut the dough into two equal portions. Place one portion between two sheets of wax or parchment paper and use a rolling pin to roll it out to a thickness of about 2 mm. Cut into large, imperfect rectangles and arrange them on half of the prepared baking sheet. Repeat with the second portion of dough, filling up the other half of the baking sheet. Prick each rectangle with a fork two or three times. Bake until the edges are toasted, 12 to 15 minutes, rotating the pan in the oven halfway through. Transfer to a wire rack to cool and crisp. (Store the crisps in an airtight container for up to 1 week.)

7. Arrange the trout fillet on a nice-looking wood cutting board and sprinkle with the dill. Heap some of the pickled cabbage in a small serving bowl. Put the crème fraîche in another small serving bowl and set them both on the board with a small fork and spoon for serving. Scatter the rye crisps around the board and serve.

OUR RECOMMENDED BREWS:

Red's Rye IPA FOUNDERS BREWING CO. / **Cane & Ebel Rye** TWO BROTHERS BREWING CO. / **Six** UPRIGHT BREWING / **Hop Rod Rye** BEAR REPUBLIC / **Rye Pale Ale** TERRAPIN

CHICKEN, PEACH, AND ZUCCHINI KEBABS
WITH MINT SALSA VERDE

BELGIAN ALE WITH PEACHES

MEET YOUR SUMMER BBQ UPGRADE. Every July and August, a ripe, juicy peach can set the beauty of the entire season in the palm of your hand. Craft brewers have long wanted to capture that in beer, as well—the luscious flavor, the fleeting perfection. In Belgium, peach lambics have been around for some time; more recently, many American craft brewers have embarked on peachy brewing projects, especially with bigger-flavored Belgian-style and sour beers, which have the heft and spice to offset both the sweet peach fruit and the peachy-tasting hops well.

Like the fruit that inspires them, the supply of these seasonal beers is limited, so act fast if you see one; it will surely sell out. Once you score, it's time to grill out. With these fun, easy kebabs, the flavors of caramelized peaches and strong peach beers go hand in hand with every bite, and the zingy flavors of the salsa verde pop against the spicy hops. Beers to look for include those literally made with peaches—avoid like the plague large commercial brands with imitation peach flavor!—and, if you're willing to do the research, any beers with strong Citra, Simcoe, or Nelson Sauvin hops from New Zealand, all of which exhibit strong aromas and flavors of summer's best, brightest fruit.

Serves 6 to 8

1 CUP/30 G LOOSELY PACKED FRESH MINT LEAVES

1 CUP/20 G LOOSELY PACKED FRESH PARSLEY LEAVES

5 GARLIC CLOVES, CRUSHED

½ TSP RED PEPPER FLAKES

FINE SEA SALT AND FRESHLY GROUND BLACK PEPPER

½ CUP/120 ML EXTRA-VIRGIN OLIVE OIL

2 LB/910 G BONELESS, SKINLESS CHICKEN THIGHS, CUT INTO 1-IN/2.5-CM PIECES

2 SMALL ZUCCHINI, SLICED VERY THINLY INTO RIBBONS LENGTHWISE ON A MANDOLINE OR WITH A VEGETABLE PEELER

4 LARGE PEACHES, HALVED, PITTED, AND CUT INTO 1-IN/2.5-CM CHUNKS

2 LEMONS, HALVED CROSSWISE

1. Combine the mint, parsley, garlic, red pepper flakes, 1 tsp salt, and ½ tsp pepper in a food processor and pulse until the herbs and garlic are finely chopped. Drizzle in the olive oil and pulse just to combine into a salsa verde.

2. Pour about half of the salsa verde into a medium bowl, add the chicken pieces, season generously with more salt, and toss to coat. (Add a little more of the salsa verde if needed to coat well.) Cover and let marinate in the refrigerator for at least 2 hours, or preferably overnight. Pour the rest of the salsa verde into a small bowl, cover, and refrigerate until ready to serve.

CONTINUED

3. About 1 hour before grilling, soak twenty 6-in/ 15-cm bamboo skewers in water to cover. Prepare a medium-hot fire in a charcoal grill or preheat a gas grill to medium-high.

4. While the grill is heating, assemble the kebabs. Drain the skewers. Spear a piece of chicken on a skewer, followed by a zucchini ribbon, folding it up on the skewer so it's about the same width as the chicken piece. Next, add a peach chunk. Repeat the trio one more time, and then end with a third piece of chicken. Repeat to assemble the remaining skewers. You should have enough for 18 to 20 skewers, each loaded with three pieces of chicken, two peach chunks, and two folded zucchini ribbons. Brush the kebabs, especially the peaches and zucchini, with any marinade left in the bowl, and season all over with salt and pepper.

5. Arrange the kebabs over the hottest part of the grill and cook, turning once, until nicely grill-marked on both sides, 3 to 4 minutes per side. Move the skewers to a cooler part of the grill (the edges of a charcoal grill or the top rack of a gas grill) and place the lemon halves on the hot area, cut-side down. Cover the grill and cook until the chicken is opaque throughout and the lemons are charred, 2 to 3 minutes longer.

6. Arrange the kebabs on a large platter and drizzle with the reserved salsa verde. Serve with the grilled lemons on the platter for squeezing.

OUR RECOMMENDED BREWS:

Brainless on Peaches Belgian-Style Ale EPIC BREWING CO. / Avant Pêche ODELL / Peach Grand Cru GREAT DIVIDE / Peche 'n Brett LOGSDON FARMHOUSE ALES / Brandy Barrel Pêche ALMANAC

BRATWURST EN CROUTE
WITH SPICED ALE MUSTARD

WEIZENBOCK

IS THERE A MORE ICONIC PAIR THAN BEER AND BRATWURST? Summer memories are made of throwing brats on the grill, but in our year-round version, the classic German staple is cooked first in a bath of brew, then baked in a coat of flaky puff pastry and served up with a rich beer mustard spiced with fennel seeds and caraway seeds that may well become your new favorite condiment. Every component of this recipe is far easier than the finished dish will allow your friends to believe. And they *will* be asking for that mustard recipe.

While many a beer goes well with brats, we looked back to Germany and a sometimes over-looked style, weizenbock, a soft and spicy brew with a touch of clove that works well with the flavorful mustard. Weizenbocks come in a wide array of hues, from a coppery to a woody brown, and tend to exhibit a bit of dark fruit and bready flavors. There are many excellent versions available; consider releases from Weihenstephaner, Hopf, and the famous Old World/New World collaboration, Brooklyn & Schneider Hopfenweisse.

Serves 4 to 6

BRATWURST EN CROUTE

2 CUPS/480 ML AMBER ALE

4 BRATWURST

1 SHEET FROZEN PUFF PASTRY DOUGH, THAWED ACCORDING TO PACKAGE DIRECTIONS

1 LARGE EGG BEATEN WITH 1 TBSP WATER, FOR AN EGG WASH

POPPYSEEDS FOR SPRINKLING

SPICED ALE MUSTARD

1 TBSP FENNEL SEEDS

1 TBSP MUSTARD SEEDS

½ TBSP CARAWAY SEEDS

4 EGG YOLKS

2 TBSP LIGHT BROWN SUGAR

⅓ CUP/80 ML MALT VINEGAR

¼ CUP/60 ML AMBER ALE

3 TBSP DRY YELLOW MUSTARD POWDER

1 TSP FINE SEA SALT

DASH OF WORCESTERSHIRE SAUCE

1. **TO MAKE THE BRATWURST EN CROUTE:** Preheat the oven to 400°F/200°C. Line a rimmed baking sheet with parchment paper.

2. Bring the ale to a simmer over high heat in a 2-qt/2-L pot. (Watch carefully so it doesn't boil over.) Add the bratwurst and return to a simmer. Lower the heat to maintain a low simmer, cover partially, and cook until the bratwurst are firm and cooked through, 10 to 12 minutes. Remove the bratwurst from the ale and set aside to cool and dry. (Discard the ale.)

3. Roll out the puff pastry on a lightly floured work surface into a 10-in/25-cm square. Cut the pastry into four equal smaller squares. Roll up each brat in a square of dough. Pinch the seams together and set the wrapped brats on the prepared baking sheet at least 2 in/5 cm apart. Brush the dough lightly with the egg wash and sprinkle generously with poppyseeds. Bake until the pastry is golden brown and, well, puffy, 25 to 30 minutes.

4. **TO MAKE THE MUSTARD:** Fill a medium saucepan with about 1½ in/4 cm of water and bring to a boil over high heat. Lower the heat to maintain a low simmer.

5. Meanwhile, place a small, heavy, dry skillet over medium-high heat. Add the fennel seeds, mustard seeds, and caraway seeds to the pan and toast, swirling the pan constantly, until the seeds are fragrant and lightly browned, about 1 minute. Transfer the seeds to a mortar and pestle or a spice grinder and grind to a fine powder.

6. Beat the egg yolks with the brown sugar in a large, nonreactive metal bowl. Whisk in the ground spice mixture, vinegar, ale, mustard powder, salt, and Worcestershire sauce. Set the bowl over the pot of gently simmering water, making sure that the water does not touch the bottom of the bowl. Cook the mixture, gently whisking constantly, until it thickens to a loose mustard consistency, 3 to 5 minutes. (Note: The mustard will continue to thicken as it cools, so remove it from the heat when it is slightly runnier than you want it to be in the end.) Remove the bowl from the heat and let the mustard cool to room temperature, stirring often to prevent a skin from forming. Transfer the mustard to a serving bowl or jar. (The mustard will keep, covered in the refrigerator, for up to 5 days.)

7. Cut the hot bratwurst en croute into thick slices and arrange them on a platter. Serve immediately, with the mustard on the side for dolloping, spreading, or dipping.

OUR RECOMMENDED BREWS:

Vitus WEIHENSTEPHANER / Aventinus SCHNEIDER / Hopfenweisse BROOKLYN & SCHNEIDER / Moonglow Weizenbock VICTORY / Shawinigan Handshake LE TROU DU DIABLE

RASPBERRY LIÈGE WAFFLES

FRAMBOISE

LIÈGE WAFFLES ARE THE ULTIMATE BELGIAN WAFFLE, ORIGINALLY HAILING FROM THE CITY OF THE SAME NAME, A LITTLE OVER AN HOUR EAST OF BRUSSELS. Made from an egg-rich yeast dough, these are denser, richer, and, dare we say, more delicious than typical Americanized versions of Belgian waffles. The key ingredient in Liège waffles is pearl sugar, a large-crystal sugar that won't melt in the waffle iron, giving them a pleasing crunch inside. An additional sprinkle of granulated sugar creates a caramelized exterior. Look for Belgian pearl sugar at specialty baking supply stores, or order it online from Lars' Own (www.larsown.com).

The ultimate beer to go with your raspberry-flecked Liège waffle is framboise, the tart, winelike beer made from lambic (the world-famous sour, wild-yeast beer of the region) and raspberries. Beware of popular commercial versions that are artificially sweetened with an additive that cannot be metabolized by wild yeasts; this keeps the beer perpetually sweet, as belief persists that Americans won't drink it any other way.

We disagree, preferring tarter, more angular versions that are much more interesting tasting and present another fascinating set of flavors with complementary foods, like these berry-flecked waffles. Wisconsin's New Glarus, the first American brewery to age beer in huge oak casks that formerly held wine, is famous for its cherry and raspberry sour beers, including Raspberry Tart, which uses ¾ lb/340 g of Oregon raspberries in *every bottle*. You might have to make a trip to the Heartland to try this beer, but you would be joining a great American beer pilgrimage in the process.

For another take on the style, Mikkeller's Spontan-framboos pops with a tart-sweet, Lambrusco-like tang and effervescence. Also look for Lost Abbey's superb Framboise de Amarosa, Cantillon's very tart Rosé de Gambrinus, or other traditional wild ales using raspberries.

Makes 6 to 8 waffles

¼ CUP/60 ML WARM WATER (100° TO 115°F/ 38° TO 45°C)

1½ TSP ACTIVE DRY YEAST

1 TBSP GRANULATED SUGAR, PLUS MORE FOR SPRINKLING

1 CUP/120 G ALL-PURPOSE FLOUR

½ CUP/60 G WHOLE-WHEAT FLOUR

5 LARGE EGGS

1½ TSP PURE VANILLA EXTRACT

½ TSP FINE SEA SALT

½ CUP/110 G UNSALTED BUTTER, MELTED

¼ CUP/50 G PEARL SUGAR (SEE RECIPE INTRODUCTION), OR SUGAR CUBES PULVERIZED INTO PEA-SIZE PIECES IN A FOOD PROCESSOR

6 OZ/170 G FRESH RASPBERRIES

1. Put the warm water in a small bowl and whisk in the yeast, then the 1 Tbsp granulated sugar until dissolved. Set aside until foamy, 5 to 7 minutes.

2. Meanwhile, sift the all-purpose flour and whole-wheat flour together into a medium bowl. Whisk together the eggs, vanilla, and salt in another medium bowl until well blended. Add the egg mixture to the flours, along with the yeast mixture and melted butter, and whisk the thick batter until relatively smooth. Cover the bowl with plastic wrap and set aside in a warm place until doubled in size, about 1½ hours. (You can also let the batter rise in the refrigerator overnight.)

3. Fold the pearl sugar and raspberries into the batter until evenly distributed. Cover and set aside to rest for about 15 minutes. Preheat a Belgian-style waffle maker to medium-high heat.

4. Lightly butter the top and bottom of the waffle maker. Scoop ½ to ¾ cup/120 to 180 ml of the batter into the center of the waffle maker, spread it a bit to distribute the raspberries evenly, and quickly sprinkle the top with about ¾ tsp granulated sugar. Close the lid and cook until the waffle maker's indicator says it is done, or until deeply browned and crisp, 2 to 4 minutes.

5. Transfer the waffle to a plate and repeat to cook the remaining waffles. The goal is to produce medium-size waffles with jagged edges, not perfectly round ones, so adjust the amount of batter per waffle as needed. If the raspberries leave burned bits in the waffle maker, carefully wipe it clean with paper towels. The waffles are best after cooling for about 10 minutes, or even to room temperature, to allow the caramelized sugar on the outside to crisp slightly.

6. Serve the waffles wrapped in squares of parchment paper, as you would get from a Belgian street cart. No forks needed! (The waffles are most delicious within a couple hours of cooking, but can be wrapped tightly in plastic and refrigerated for up to 2 days. Reheat in the oven before serving.)

OUR RECOMMENDED BREWS:

Raspberry Tart NEW GLARUS / Spontanframboos MIKKELLER / Framboise de Amarosa LOST ABBEY / Rosé de Gambrinus BRASSERIE CANTILLON / Raspberry Lambic UPLAND

FRUIT BEER FLOAT

AMERICAN WILD & SOUR ALE WITH FRUIT

WILD AND SOUR ALES, BEERS MADE WITH WILD YEASTS THAT IMPART APPEALING ACIDITY DEVELOPED OVER EXTENDED TIME SPENT EITHER IN STEEL TANKS OR WOOD BARRELS, ARE A JOY TO PAIR WITH THE RIGHT FOODS. American craft brewers, inspired by Belgian masters, began tinkering with the styles in earnest in the early 1990s, adding fruits and laying the domestic foundations for a bona fide movement in craft beer.

Today, American wild and sour ales hold their own with the best in the world. By playing up acidity and fruity notes instead of bitterness, wild-yeast brewers have won over scores of drinkers who thought they'd never, ever like craft beer. Like the Belgian lambics that inspired them, these beers are often named for their fruity additions using Dutch or French: cherry (*kriek*), raspberry (*framboise*), apple (*pomme*), black currant (*cassis*), and peach (*pêche*). For the distinctive tang, many of these complex, almost winelike sour beers use *Lactobacillus*, the same bacteria strain that makes yogurt's pleasantly sour taste so appealing.

In this ideal summertime pairing, we went against the conventional wisdom about beer floats, which recommends using stouts and porters. We found that the bitterness in stout fights ice cream to the death. Instead, look to fruit; we discovered that the very same lactic flavor in sour beer works magic when a scoop of good vanilla ice cream is launched in. One beer in particular took the cake, or rather the ice cream—Bier Royale from The Commons, in Portland, Oregon, which is flavored liberally with black currants and has a gorgeous rosy hue. Is this beer simply too good to mix with ice cream? We have to say no; we love its bracing bite all on its own, but we also love what happens when that bite meets another mouthful of frozen creamy goodness. The beer foam and ice cream form a soft cap, like an edible science experiment, while the sweet cream and tart beer trade high fives of flavor. It's summertime in a glass, whatever the weather.

Serves 1

¾ CUP/180 ML AMERICAN WILD ALE WITH FRUIT
1 GIANT SCOOP GOOD-QUALITY VANILLA ICE CREAM
RASPBERRIES FOR GARNISH (OPTIONAL)

Pour the ale into a stemmed tulip glass. Carefully slip in the scoop of ice cream. It's important to add the ice cream to the beer, rather than vice versa, to ensure that it will float and not stick to the bottom of the glass. Garnish with two or three raspberries, if desired. Serve immediately with a spoon and straw.

OUR RECOMMENDED BREWS:

Bier Royale THE COMMONS BREWERY / **Kriek** CASCADE BARREL HOUSE / **Rainier Kriek** DOUBLE MOUNTAIN / **Festina Pêche** DOGFISH HEAD / **Atrial Rubicite** JESTER KING

Chapter 3

HOPPY & HERBAL

To craft this eclectic group of recipes, we took on the challenge of pairing what is surely the most formidable beer flavor of all: bitterness, also the most prominent taste in two of craft beer's most popular categories, pale ale and IPA.

Harvested in fall and dried in kilns, hops are to beer what grapes are to wine in some respects: distinct varietals that have an integral effect on how the final beer will taste and smell.

Hops have been added to beer since the Middle Ages, but amazingly, experimentation with them in beer making continues to reach new heights. There are now ultra-hoppy adaptations of styles that express little of the plants' green, herbaceous flavors. This might seem contradictory, but think of it this way: It's like an orange peel, which, when squeezed, smells as sweet and juicy as sherbet. Now bite into the rind and chew. So goes the hop, whose secretions, in the form of fatty acids, impart varying degrees of hop flavor to beer, from grassy, citrusy, and floral to astringently piney and even weedlike (as in "dank," as some are described). It all depends on how and when the hops are added to the beer and in what exact form and quantities. There are even hop extracts added to certain very famous beers (like Russian River's Pliny the Elder) that push the green factor to "11" without the unpleasant vegetal side effects that overhopped beers can have. For a truly vivid experience of what hops can do to beer, try a fresh-hop ale after fall's big harvests.

Hoppy beers are everywhere, and run the gamut of styles these days. There are traditionally mellow English bitters, new-school English bitters, and IPAs of many stripes (like the coriander-kissed "white" IPAs found on page 81). The range of hops brewers have to choose from is likewise vast; there are well over thirty common commercial varieties, used in myriad combinations. Hops grown in different soils clearly exhibit deep differences in flavor and aroma. Call it *beeroir*.

To the home chef eager to pair hoppy beer styles with food, we caution that the proposition can be a bit problematic. While agreeably found in foods like bitter greens (for example, radicchio and rapini) citrus peel, walnuts, chocolate, and coffee, in beer, bitterness can be aspirin-like in excess, wrestling delicate food flavors to the mat and then taunting them, mercilessly, with an acrid aftertaste.

One key we discovered in our test kitchen is the way that very hoppy beers tend to meet (and sometimes enhance) foods with a good amount of acid, with each powerful taste bringing the other into balance. Also, dishes loaded with fragrant herbs, like the oregano in our take on Stromboli (page 79), are matched by the herbal qualities in some hoppy brews. And these beers have the power to stand up to spicy heat, while any residual sweetness and tang simultaneously nudge notoriously shy umami to center stage.

UMAMI EDAMAME

AMERICAN-STYLE INDIA PALE ALE

LED BY WEST COAST BREWERS BASED NEAR THE HOP-GROWING REGIONS OF THE YAKIMA AND WILLAMETTE VALLEYS, THE IPA CRAZE OF THE 1990S AND 2000S AT TIMES PUSHED BREWERS, HOPS GROWERS, AND CONSUMERS TO THE BRINK. There were hops-supply contract disputes and shortages, and mutterings about a hops "arms race" that was leading brewers to oversaturate their beers with such pungent levels of resinous hops that they practically numb the face. (Hence the rather dubious invention of "triple IPA.") But the pendulum swung back, and a distinctly West Coast, some would say "American," style of IPA emerged.

Whereas English IPA tends, at least historically, to employ more caramel malts—literally, malts roasted to a caramel color and flavor—to add heft and balance hop bitterness, "American IPA" lowers those malts a notch, playing down core bitterness, avoiding an aspiriny taste, and increasing juicy, floral, and refreshing flavors by means of massive late additions of hops during the all-important boiling stage. It's a bit like that bright squeeze of fresh lemon on *bistecca Fiorentina*. There are many excellent American-style IPAs, from the readily available Lagunitas IPA and Sierra Nevada Torpedo Extra IPA to regional favorites like Odell IPA, Alpine Brewing Company's Duet, and Half Acre & Three Floyds' Anicca.

These beers are a sociable lot, simply because they're less likely to drub the palate into submission. They can even be used as icebreakers (but watch out, they're about 30 percent stronger than most of the beers in chapter 1). As for the ultimate party-starter, seasoned soybeans in the shell are one of the all-time easiest, most satisfying welcome nibbles you can put on the table.

Enter "umami edamame." In this simple but exceptionally flavorful preparation, the bitter and bright, fruity qualities of India pale ale magnify the umami (see page 18) of the soy sauce and contrast the spicy flavors of the stir-fried dressing made with chiles, garlic, and ginger. Keep bags of frozen edamame in your freezer to make this dish for a spontaneous snack, but searching out fresh edamame, found at some farmers' markets and Asian grocers, is even better.

Serves 4 to 6

1 LB/455 G FRESH OR FROZEN EDAMAME IN THEIR PODS

1½ TBSP SOY SAUCE

1 TSP SUGAR

1 TBSP PEANUT OIL OR VEGETABLE OIL

3 TO 5 WHOLE SMALL DRIED CHILES SUCH AS THAI BIRD'S-EYE, CAYENNE, OR CHILE DE ÁRBOL

3 GARLIC CLOVES, MINCED

1 TBSP PEELED AND MINCED FRESH GINGER

1. Cook the edamame in a large pot of boiling water until just softened, about 4 minutes. Drain and pat dry.

2. Mix together the soy sauce and sugar in a small bowl. Have all the other ingredients at the ready (stir-frying is quick work!).

3. Heat the peanut oil in a wok or large sauté pan over medium-high heat until you just begin to see wisps of smoke. Add the chiles, garlic, and ginger and stir-fry until softened, about 1 minute; lower the heat if anything begins to char. Stir in the edamame to coat in the oil. Add the soy sauce mixture and stir-fry until the sauce thickens and clings to the edamame, about 30 seconds. Transfer to a platter and serve immediately, with a small bowl for discarded shells.

OUR RECOMMENDED BREWS:

IPA LAGUNITAS; ODELL; BREAKSIDE BREWERY **/ Anicca** HALF ACRE & THREE FLOYDS **/ Duet** ALPINE **/ Torpedo Extra** SIERRA NEVADA **/ ReAle Extra** BIRRA DEL BORGO

BLISTERED PADRÓN PEPPER PINTXOS

SESSION IPA

A GREAT HORS D'OEUVRE FILLS A KITCHEN WITH AROMAS, STIRS APPETITES, AND SPURS A PARTY TO INSTANT CONVERSATION. So it is with these flash-fried Spanish peppers, and a great beer to go with them. Padrón peppers, a beautiful and poppable small green variety, are usually mild, but every once in a while you'll get a spicy one, making this an even more exciting snack to serve with "session beers"—lower-alcohol brews meant for easy nights of long conversation.

Similar to the Japanese shishito pepper (a suitable substitute), Padrón peppers are a bite-size tradition from the *pintxos*, or tapas, world, the sort that line the counters of bars in Spain's vibrant Basque country. They develop delicious sweet, smoky, and bitter flavors when they hit a scalding pan.

The right beer for this simple bite is either a session IPA or the very closely related American pale ale (APA), which cool the mouth and refresh but are far from lacking in character, with a tang of aromatic hops but less of the bitter background (and alcohol) of bigger IPAs. The aromatic, tropical, fruity notes of these lighter brews accent the ripe, fleshy flavors exploding from the blistered peppers, while the clean-finishing dryness resets the palate. One of the best we've ever tried is called Reiner, at 2.8% ABV, which goes down easily again and again. It's obscure, but the best East Coast bottle shops will stock it.

Serves 6 to 8

2 TBSP EXTRA-VIRGIN OLIVE OIL, PLUS MORE FOR DRIZZLING

8 OZ/225 G PADRÓN PEPPERS (ABOUT 30)

FINE SEA SALT

8 THICK SLICES COUNTRY-STYLE BREAD

4 OZ/115 G FROMAGE BLANC OR CHÈVRE

COARSE, FLAKY SEA SALT, SUCH AS MALDON, FOR SPRINKLING

1. Heat the olive oil over medium-high heat in a large skillet, preferably cast iron. When it just begins to smoke, add the peppers and sauté until they collapse and blacken in spots, about 5 minutes. Season with a big pinch of fine sea salt, toss to coat, and transfer the peppers to a plate.

2. Working in batches, toast the bread slices in the skillet until charred on both sides but still soft in the middle, 1 to 2 minutes per side; adjust the heat as needed to cook the slices evenly, and drizzle the pan with a little more olive oil if it seems dry.

3. Spread a thick layer of the fromage blanc on each hot toasted bread slice. Top with the peppers, dividing them evenly. Drizzle with olive oil, sprinkle generously with coarse sea salt, and serve immediately.

OUR RECOMMENDED BREWS:

Reiner MONTSENY / **All Day IPA** FOUNDERS / **River Ale** DESCHUTES BREWERY / **Alpha Session Ale** DRAKE'S / **Boat Beer** CARTON

DAY-GLO DEVILED EGGS

BELGIAN ALE

FORGET THOSE ALIEN-LOOKING, DECOMPOSING ORBS THAT FLOAT OMINOUSLY IN GLASS JARS AT OLD-SCHOOL BARS, MORE A DARE THAN APPETIZING INVITATION. In this easily manageable recipe, the classic pickled-egg bar snack gets gussied up in a striking, completely natural coat of neon yellow, blowing away expectations for the ubiquitous hors d'oeuvre. With the rich, yolky, mustard-and-chile-tinged taste here, it's important to choose a beer with enough body, maltiness, and herbal hops to complement those flavors as well as the mingling vinegar, salt, and faintly currylike turmeric elements.

Brewery Ommegang's mellow-tasting Belgian ale Rare Vos, a moderately hoppy, copper-hued brew with additions of sweet orange peel, grains of paradise, and coriander and a nutty finish, is well-matched to the task. Another great beer in this realm is Orval, one of the classic Trappist ales of Belgium, which has the distinction of being one of the first beers redolent of *Brettanomyces*—the wild, leathery, funky yeast strain—to become popular in the United States.

Makes 16 deviled eggs

1 CUP/240 ML CIDER VINEGAR

2 JALAPEÑO CHILES, THINLY SLICED

2 GARLIC CLOVES, THINLY SLICED

1 TBSP YELLOW MUSTARD SEEDS

1 TBSP FINE SEA SALT

1 TBSP SUGAR

1 TSP GROUND TURMERIC

8 LARGE EGGS

¾ CUP/180 ML MAYONNAISE

1 TSP DIJON MUSTARD

1. Combine the vinegar, jalapeños, garlic, mustard seeds, salt, sugar, turmeric, and 1 cup/240 ml water in a small saucepan and bring to a boil over medium-high heat, stirring occasionally. Remove from the heat and let cool to room temperature.

2. Meanwhile, bring a medium pot of water to a boil over high heat. Lower the eggs into the boiling water with a slotted spoon, and set a timer for 13 minutes. Adjust the heat as needed to maintain a gentle simmer as the eggs cook. When the timer goes off, drain the eggs and transfer them to a large bowl of ice water to cool completely. Peel the eggs under cold running water and put them in a container that will hold them and the pickling brine comfortably, such as a 1-qt/960-ml glass jar.

3. Pour the cooled brine, solids and all, over the peeled eggs and push the eggs down to submerge. Cover and refrigerate for 8 to 12 hours to allow the eggs to pick up the color and flavor of the brine.

4. Drain the eggs and other solids, discarding the brine but reserving all the pickled bits. Cut the eggs in half lengthwise and carefully pop out the yolks. Set the whites aside. Press the yolks through a ricer, food mill, or fine-mesh sieve into a medium bowl. Add the mayonnaise and mustard to the yolks and beat until smooth and fluffy. Spoon the filling mixture into a pastry bag fitted with a smooth tip, or use a resealable plastic bag and snip off a corner. Pipe the filling into the cavities of the egg whites.

5. Top each deviled egg with a slice of the pickled jalapeño and/or garlic and a tiny dollop of pickled mustard seeds. Serve immediately, or cover and refrigerate for up to 1 day.

OUR RECOMMENDED BREWS:

Rare Vos OMMEGANG / **Orval** BRASSERIE D'ORVAL / **Luciernaga** JOLLY PUMPKIN / **Lil' Devil** ALESMITH / **Matilda** GOOSE ISLAND

GLAMORGAN "SAUSAGES"

EXTRA SPECIAL BITTER

WALES, THE MUCH-ROMANTICIZED MOUNTAINOUS NATION ON GREAT BRITAIN'S GLACIATED WESTERN SHORES, IS A HEARTY, SOULFUL PLACE. Beer is the national drink; leeks are the national vegetable. Cheese isn't far behind in status—Welsh Rarebit (page 125) is another national favorite that is extremely beer-friendly. Little known in the United States, the classic Glamorgan "sausage" is named for its shape—despite the fact that it's a Cheddar-and-leek croquette without a bit of meat in it—and for the region anchored by Cardiff, entry point and capital of the nation, where this dish is found on many a pub and restaurant menu.

What makes this easy vegetarian dish so fun and rewarding is how much truly greater it is than the sum of its parts. The texture alone is appealing, with an ample crunch and toothsome interior. Pass as an hors d'oeuvre or serve two on a plate as a tapas or side. Served warm, with a dollop of English mustard, the crisp croquettes are already a treat; but add in a glass of moderately hoppy English-style pale ale or an ESB ("Extra Special Bitter," derived from English malted barley) and you have a quintessential pairing in hand.

ESB is another super-versatile style. With medium to fairly high bitterness, a distinct caramel-malt sweetness, and nutty, biscuity flavors, ESB is generally low to medium in alcohol content, and may have a bit of mineral flavor, from hard brewing water. Overall, the best are balanced, moderate, and highly drinkable.

Serves 4 to 8

2 LARGE LEEKS

2 TBSP UNSALTED BUTTER

5 OZ/150 G CAERPHILLY CHEESE OR ANY ENGLISH CHEDDAR, FINELY SHREDDED

1 CUP/110 G COARSE, DRIED BREAD CRUMBS, PREFERABLY HOMEMADE OR PANKO

2 TBSP FINELY CHOPPED FRESH PARSLEY

1 TSP CHOPPED FRESH THYME

2 LARGE EGGS, PLUS 2 EGG WHITES

1 TSP ENGLISH MUSTARD, PLUS MORE FOR DIPPING

¼ TSP FRESHLY GROUND PEPPER

PEANUT OIL OR VEGETABLE OIL FOR FRYING

1. Trim the roots and dark green tops from the leeks. Halve them lengthwise, then thinly slice crosswise. Put the sliced leeks in a large bowl and fill it with cold water. Swish the leeks around to remove any sand or dirt. The leeks will float to the surface of the water and the dirt will fall to the bottom; skim the leeks from the top and transfer them to a salad spinner or kitchen towel and dry.

2. Melt the butter in a sauté pan over medium-low heat. Add the leeks and sauté until soft and just beginning to color, 8 to 10 minutes. Remove from the heat and let cool.

3. Stir together the cooled leeks, cheese, ½ cup/ 55 g of the bread crumbs, the parsley, and thyme in a large bowl. Beat the 2 whole eggs with the mustard and pepper in a separate bowl. Stir the egg mixture into the leek mixture until well combined. Divide the mixture into eight equal portions and roll each into a fat sausage-shaped croquette. Place the croquettes on a plate, cover loosely with plastic wrap, and refrigerate for about 30 minutes.

4. Beat the egg whites lightly in a bowl until just frothy. Put the remaining ½ cup/55 g bread crumbs in a shallow bowl. Dip the croquettes, one at a time, into the beaten egg whites, then roll them in the bread crumbs, patting to help the crumbs adhere and coat evenly. Return the breaded croquettes to the plate, re-cover, and return to the refrigerator for at least 30 minutes, or up to 24 hours.

5. Pour peanut oil into a large skillet to a depth of ½ in/12 mm and heat over medium-high heat. When the oil reaches 325°F/165°C, or when a bread crumb sizzles enthusiastically, carefully add about half of the croquettes (or fewer; you don't want to overcrowd the pan). Fry, turning once, until deep golden on both sides, 2 to 3 minutes per side. Transfer the croquettes to a platter lined with paper towels and repeat to fry the rest. Adjust the heat as needed to maintain the oil temperature, and allow it to return to 325°F/165°C between batches.

6. Serve the croquettes immediately, with mustard for dipping.

OUR RECOMMENDED BREWS:

DBA FIRESTONE WALKER / **London Pride** FULLER'S / **5 Barrel Pale Ale** ODELL / **The Wise ESB** ELYSIAN / **Sawtooth Ale** LEFTHAND

HOT REUBEN DIP

RYE PALE OR RYE IPA

THE INSPIRATION FOR THIS CROWD-PLEASING TAKE ON HOT ARTICHOKE DIP COMES FROM ONE OF THE WORLD'S BEST PUB SANDWICHES, THE MOUNTAIN OF SAVORY CORNED BEEF, TANGY SAUERKRAUT, AND RUSSIAN DRESSING BETWEEN TWO SLICES OF RYE BREAD OTHERWISE KNOWN AS A REUBEN. With its soft but substantial texture, the dip rendition practically dares you not to take repeated bites.

Once it comes out of the oven, everyone will gather round this creamy, molten magic and scramble for the two-bite rye toasts, so you'll need plenty of beer to go with it. It only makes sense to start with a rye beer; the fatty, salty flavors of corned beef work surprisingly well with rye pale ale or IPA, with a touch of extra-hoppy bite and spicy rye that meld deliciously with every dip and dunk. Rye beers come in a wide range; why not try a few?

***

Serves 6 to 8

8 OZ/225 G JARLSBERG OR SWISS CHEESE, SHREDDED

4 OZ/115 G CREAM CHEESE, AT ROOM TEMPERATURE

½ CUP/120 ML MAYONNAISE

1 CUP/150 G DRAINED SAUERKRAUT

4 OZ/115 G CORNED BEEF, CHOPPED

¼ CUP/40 G MINCED DILL PICKLES

1 TBSP HEINZ CHILI SAUCE OR KETCHUP

1 TSP CARAWAY SEEDS, LIGHTLY CRUSHED IN A MORTAR WITH A PESTLE OR IN A SPICE GRINDER

¼ TSP FRESHLY GROUND BLACK PEPPER

COCKTAIL RYE BREAD, SLICED AND TOASTED, FOR SERVING

1. Preheat the oven to 350°F/180°C.

2. Beat together the shredded cheese, cream cheese, and mayonnaise in a medium bowl. Stir in the sauerkraut, corned beef, pickles, chili sauce, caraway seeds, and pepper until well combined.

3. Spread the mixture in an attractive shallow baking dish. (At this point, the dip can be baked immediately, or cover and refrigerate for up to 2 days before baking.) Bake until bubbly and lightly browned on top, 25 to 30 minutes. Serve the dip hot with the rye toasts.

VARIATION: REUBEN CANAPÉS

For a more polished presentation, spread the dip mixture on about 30 slices of cocktail rye bread (untoasted) and arrange them on two large rimmed baking sheets. Bake in a 300°F/150°C oven until the topping is melted and a bit crusty and the bread is toasted, 25 to 30 minutes, rotating the pans halfway through. Garnish the canapés with halved cornichons before serving.

OUR RECOMMENDED BREWS:

Righteous Ale SIXPOINT / **Mosaic Single Hopped Rye Ale** TERRAPIN / **Divided Sky Rye IPA** FOUR HANDS / **Bittersweet Lenny's RIPA** HE'BREW

CHORIZO PÂTÉ

AMERICAN-STYLE INDIA PALE ALE

THROUGHOUT OUR TESTS AND TASTES, WE FOUND THAT FEW FOODS PAIR EASILY WITH TANGY, FLORAL, BITTER AMERICAN-STYLE INDIA PALE ALE. But luckily, chorizo is one of them. In this quick, unusual preparation inspired by Catalan *sobrassada*—a cured pork sausage heavily spiced with paprika from the Balearic Islands off of Spain—a fiery, tangy-sour blend of spices becomes a rich, mouth-watering pâté to spread on toasted bread or spoon into celery sticks.

Choose a very good-quality dry-cured Spanish chorizo—not the raw Mexican style—but one that is still somewhat soft and tender, not extremely dry and hard, as the desired consistency is a thick, spreadable paste when it emerges from the food processor.

There are few beer styles with as many variations as IPA, so get ready to explore. In this case, our vote for best bet is a citrusy, assertive American IPA.

1. Combine the chorizo, butter, vinegar, paprika, thyme, salt, and black pepper in a food processor and process to a relatively smooth purée, stopping to scrape down the sides of the bowl as needed.

2. Pack the pâté into a wide-mouth glass jam jar, preferably one with a hinged lid, cover, and refrigerate to allow the flavors to meld, at least 1 hour. (The pâté will keep, tightly covered in the refrigerator, for up to 1 week.)

3. Remove the pâté from the refrigerator about 1 hour before serving to bring it to room temperature. Preheat a grill pan or a gas grill to high. Drizzle the bread slices lightly with olive oil and arrange them in the grill pan or on the grill rack, working in batches as needed, and toast until nicely charred, with grill marks, 1 to 2 minutes per side.

4. Serve the pâté spread on the grilled bread and spooned into celery sticks, topped with pickled peppers. Alternatively, you can arrange the jar of pâté, grilled bread, celery sticks, and a small dish of peppers on a large platter and have your guests assemble bites themselves.

Serves 6 to 8

6 OZ/170 G SPANISH CURED CHORIZO, CASING REMOVED AND THICKLY SLICED

½ CUP/110 G UNSALTED BUTTER, AT ROOM TEMPERATURE

2 TBSP SHERRY VINEGAR

2 TSP SWEET OR HOT PAPRIKA

2 TSP FRESH THYME LEAVES

½ TSP FINE SEA SALT

½ TSP FRESHLY GROUND BLACK PEPPER

1 SMALL LOAF COUNTRY-STYLE BREAD, CUT INTO ½-IN/12-MM SLICES

EXTRA-VIRGIN OLIVE OIL FOR DRIZZLING

CELERY STICKS FOR SERVING

PICKLED PIPARRA OR BANANA PEPPERS FOR SERVING

OUR RECOMMENDED BREWS:

Sculpin IPA BALLAST POINT / **Blind Pig IPA** RUSSIAN RIVER / **Two Hearted Ale** BELL'S / **Beer Lunch** MAINE BEER COMPANY / **Nugget Nectar** TROEG'S

BRUSSELS SPROUTS AND TALEGGIO PIZZA
WITH MELTING SPECK

AMERICAN PALE ALE

PIZZA MAY ETERNALLY DUEL BRATWURST FOR THE TITLE OF MOST OBVIOUS BEER COMPANION, BUT FOR THE DEDICATED HOME CONNOISSEUR THROWING A PAIRING PARTY, IT'S NOT AS EASY AS IT MIGHT SEEM: TOMATOES, ESPECIALLY, TEND TO WREAK HAVOC WHEN PAIRED WITH BEER. But this rustic, tomato-less pizza topped with earthy Brussels sprouts; funky, ripe-tasting Taleggio; and slightly smoky cured speck is a delicious match for beer—ideally, we thought, with American pale ale, a drier version of English pale ale. This style has a bright note of grapefruit rind, a touch of pine, and a lingering bitterness from American hops.

There are many great versions of this clean, orange-hued ale, led by the classic Sierra Nevada pale ale. On a smaller scale, Vermont's smallish but acclaimed Hill Farmstead Brewery excels in the style, with several rotating versions including the sought-after Edward.

Serves 4

1 LB/455 G PIZZA DOUGH, HOMEMADE OR STORE-BOUGHT, AT ROOM TEMPERATURE

EXTRA-VIRGIN OLIVE OIL FOR DRIZZLING

2 GARLIC CLOVES, THINLY SLICED

5 OZ/140 G TALEGGIO CHEESE, CUT INTO SMALL CUBES

3½ OZ/100 G BRUSSELS SPROUTS, VERY THINLY SLICED

PINCH OF FINE SEA SALT

6 PAPER-THIN SLICES SPECK OR PROSCIUTTO

1. Position a rack 4 in/10 cm from the top heating element if you have an electric oven, or 8 in/20 cm for gas. Place a pizza stone on the rack. Preheat the oven as high as it goes, 500° to 550°F/260° to 290°C, for about 1 hour to heat the stone.

2. Just before shaping and topping the pizza, switch the oven to the broil setting. Have all of the toppings prepared.

CONTINUED

3. On a lightly floured work surface, pat the dough down and stretch it into a fat disk. Use your fingers and palms to continue pulling it wider until it's thin enough to pick up and rotate over your knuckles, gently pulling the dough and letting gravity stretch it to a large, very thin oval or rectangular shape with thicker edges. There should be some areas in the center that are so thin the light shines through. Don't be meticulous about making it perfect; leave some bubbles where the dough will blister in the oven, and it's totally okay to have areas where the dough is thicker or thinner. Just be sure to patch any holes.

4. Place the dough on a lightly floured pizza peel or rimless baking sheet as close to the edge as possible and quickly get to work on topping the pizza (if it's left on the peel too long it will become difficult to slide off). Add toppings in this order: a drizzle of olive oil; the garlic, cheese, and Brussels sprouts; and salt. Drizzle the top with a little more oil for good measure.

5. Once the toppings are added, immediately slide the pizza off the peel and onto the hot stone using swift, forward-and-back jerking motions. (This could take some practice if you haven't done it before. Basically, you want to position the pizza directly over the stone where you want it to land and then swiftly jerk the peel out from underneath it, like that old tablecloth trick where the plates and glasses remain in place. It may take a couple of jerks to release it.)

6. Broil the pizza until the crust is crisp on the bottom and blistered on top, and the Brussels sprouts are nicely charred at the edges, 5 to 7 minutes. Use the peel to rotate the pizza once about halfway through for even cooking. When the pizza is done, the crust should feel crisp when you maneuver it with the peel.

7. Transfer the pizza to a cutting board. While it's piping hot, overlap rows of the sliced speck to cover the entire surface of the pizza; the fat will gloriously melt in. Cut into wedges and serve immediately.

OUR RECOMMENDED BREWS:

Pale Ale SIERRA NEVADA / **Pale 31** FIRESTONE WALKER / **Edward** HILL FARMSTEAD / **Alpha King** THREE FLOYDS / **Daisy Cutter** HALF ACRE / **Invasion Pale Ale** CIGAR CITY

STROMBOLI
WITH SOPRESSATA, RAPINI, AND PROVOLONE

WHITE IPA

THERE ARE A NUMBER OF STORIES OFFERING THE ORIGINS OF THIS MASSIVE, AND MASSIVELY SATISFYING, ITALIAN PIZZA ROLL. Not surprisingly, all of them seem to involve the 1950 hit film *Stromboli*, starring legendarily spicy actress Ingrid Bergman. The movie wasn't about a sandwich, of course, but rather a perilous volcano off the coast of Italy. The stories make sense, given the delicious molten filling that explodes from this hearty party-pleaser.

As with pizza, pairing beer with stromboli can be tricky, so we turned to something of a trick beer: White IPA, an early-twenty-first-century variation on India pale ale that combines the herbal tang of IPA with the fruity, spicy kick of orange peel–and–coriander-spiced witbier. With its combo of citrusy, bitter, malty, and herbal flavors, it's got an answer for every flavor coming out of this version of the mountainous sandwich, especially the bittersweet rapini, bright tomatoes, and salty cheese. Chainbreaker, from Oregon's Deschutes Brewery, works especially well, light and fruity but substantial enough to stand in the spotlight.

Serves 6 to 8

1 BUNCH RAPINI, TRIMMED AND CUT INTO 2-IN/5-CM PIECES

4 TBSP/60 ML EXTRA-VIRGIN OLIVE OIL

FINE SEA SALT

ONE 28-OZ/794-G CAN WHOLE PEELED TOMATOES, PREFERABLY SAN MARZANO

2 LARGE GARLIC CLOVES, MINCED

2 TSP CHOPPED FRESH OREGANO

1 LB/455 G PIZZA DOUGH, HOMEMADE OR STORE-BOUGHT, AT ROOM TEMPERATURE

¼ CUP/30 G FRESHLY GRATED PARMIGIANO-REGGIANO CHEESE

4 OZ/115 G THINLY SLICED SOPPRESSATA

4 OZ/115 G THINLY SLICED PROVOLONE CHEESE

1 LARGE EGG, LIGHTLY BEATEN

1. Preheat the oven to 450°F/230°C.

2. Toss the rapini with 2 Tbsp of the olive oil and a big pinch of salt in a large bowl. Spread it out on two large rimmed baking sheets and roast until the stalks are tender and the leaves are lightly charred, 8 to 10 minutes, rotating the pans in the oven halfway through.

3. Squish the tomatoes with your hands into a chunky sauce in a saucepan. Stir in the garlic, oregano, remaining 2 Tbsp olive oil, and 1 tsp salt. Set aside.

CONTINUED

4. Line a clean, large rimmed baking sheet with parchment paper. Roll out the dough on a lightly floured work surface into a 16-by-12-in/40.5-by-30.5-cm rectangle, with the long edges parallel to the edge of the countertop. If it is too elastic to roll out the whole way in one shot, cover it with a kitchen towel and let rest for 10 minutes, then continue rolling.

5. Spread ½ cup/120 ml of the sauce over the surface of the dough, leaving a 1-in/2.5-cm border. Sprinkle it with the Parmigiano-Reggiano. Arrange the soppressata in an even layer over the sauce, and then layer the provolone over the soppressata. Strew the rapini over that. Brush the bare edges of the dough lightly with some of the beaten egg. Beginning at the long edge closest to you, carefully roll up the dough snugly into a cylinder (like a jelly roll). Press the seam together and tuck in the ends to completely encase the filling.

6. Place the stromboli, seam-side down, on the prepared baking sheet. Brush the top and sides lightly with the egg. Cut five diagonal slits about 2 in/5 cm apart in the top of the dough for steam vents. Bake until the crust is a deep golden brown, 25 to 30 minutes. Let the stromboli cool for at least 10 minutes before slicing.

7. Meanwhile, bring the remaining sauce to a simmer over medium heat. Transfer the stromboli to a cutting board and cut it crosswise into thick slices. Serve directly from the cutting board or on a long platter, with the remaining sauce on the side for dipping.

OUR RECOMMENDED BREWS:

Chainbreaker DESCHUTES BREWERY / **Reboot** BOULEVARD BREWING CO. / **Accumulation** NEW BELGIUM BREWING / **Whiplash White** SWEETWATER BREWING COMPANY / **Pig War White IPA** HOPWORKS URBAN BREWERY

BÁNH XÈO
WITH PORK, SHRIMP, AND LOTS OF HERBS

`BELGIAN ALE`

THIS COMPLEX VIETNAMESE STREET-FOOD DELICACY ENFOLDS A WILD MIX OF FLAVORS THAT SURPRISE AND GRATIFY THE PALATE SIX WAYS TO SUNDAY, ALL IN A DELICIOUSLY LIGHT AND FLAVORFUL CREPE. While you won't find them amid the bustling night markets of Hanoi, for the herbal, citrusy, and seafood flavors in this dish we recommend a Belgian pale ale or Belgian-style IPA, especially the delicious, faintly herbal Taras Boulba. Brewed by Brussels' renowned Brasserie de la Senne, it's a dry, grassy, and yeasty beer, with a fluffy white head and mellow honey aspect to both color and after-taste. Taras Boulba is mellow on the alcohol, too, at just 4.5% ABV; if we could have put this beer on tap in our test kitchen, we would have.

Serves 6

CREPE BATTER
1 CUP/100 G BÁNH XÈO MIX OR RICE FLOUR

1 LARGE EGG

1 TSP GROUND TURMERIC

½ TSP FINE SEA SALT

ONE 13½-OZ/400-ML CAN COCONUT MILK

¾ CUP/180 ML BELGIAN ALE

1 BUNCH GREEN ONIONS, WHITE AND LIGHT GREEN PARTS ONLY, THINLY SLICED

DIPPING SAUCE
¼ CUP/60 ML VIETNAMESE FISH SAUCE

2 TBSP FRESH LIME JUICE

2 TBSP SUGAR

1 LARGE GARLIC CLOVE, MINCED

1 TSP PEELED AND GRATED GINGER

2 TO 3 RED OR GREEN THAI CHILES, STEMMED AND THINLY SLICED

ABOUT ½ CUP/120 ML PEANUT OIL OR VEGETABLE OIL

6 OZ/170 G GROUND PORK

¼ SMALL YELLOW ONION, DICED

6 OZ/170 G MEDIUM SHRIMP, PEELED, DEVEINED, AND COARSELY CHOPPED

2 TBSP FISH SAUCE

1 TSP RED PEPPER FLAKES

8 OZ/225 G BEAN SPROUTS

LEAVES FROM 1 BUNCH FRESH MINT

LEAVES FROM 1 BUNCH FRESH CILANTRO

LEAVES FROM 1 BUNCH FRESH THAI BASIL OR DILL

1. TO MAKE THE BATTER: Whisk together the bánh xèo mix, egg, turmeric, and salt in a large bowl. Slowly pour in the coconut milk and then the ale, whisking constantly to prevent lumps. Stir in the green onions, cover, and set aside to rest for 30 minutes, or refrigerate for up to 1 day. Stir the crepe batter before using and check the consistency. It should be the thickness of heavy cream (add a little more ale if it seems too thick).

CONTINUED

2. TO MAKE THE DIPPING SAUCE: Whisk together the fish sauce, lime juice, sugar, garlic, ginger, chiles, and 2 Tbsp water in a small bowl. Set aside. (The sauce will keep, covered in the refrigerator, for up to 5 days.)

3. Preheat the oven to 200°F/95°C.

4. Heat 1 Tbsp of the peanut oil in a 10-in/25-cm nonstick sauté pan over medium-high heat. When it's shimmering, add the pork and yellow onion and cook until the pork is evenly browned and the onion is translucent, about 5 minutes. Add the shrimp, fish sauce, and red pepper flakes and sauté until the shrimp are pink and cooked through and most of the liquid has evaporated, about 5 minutes. Transfer to a bowl and set aside.

5. Wipe out the pan with paper towels and place it back over medium-high heat. Add 1 Tbsp oil. When the oil is hot, pour in about ⅓ cup/75 ml of the batter and quickly swirl it around to coat the pan until the batter stops moving and begins to set. Add about 3 Tbsp of the pork mixture and a handful of bean sprouts to half of the crepe, cover with a lid, and turn the heat to medium. Cook for 1 minute, or until the pork mixture and bean sprouts are warmed through and the edges of the crepe are browned and crisp. Remove the lid and, using a rubber spatula, carefully fold the empty half of the crepe over the fillings. Slide the crepe out of the pan onto a large rimmed baking sheet and place it in the oven to keep warm while you cook the remaining crepes. Repeat to make a total of 6 to 8 crepes.

6. Arrange the crepes on individual plates and pile a mixture of fresh mint, cilantro, and Thai basil on top of each. Divide the sauce into individual ramekins for dipping. Serve immediately.

OUR RECOMMENDED BREWS:

Taras Boulba BRASSERIE DE LA SENNE **/ XX Bitter** BROUWERIJ DE RANKE **/ Prairie Hop** PRAIRIE ARTISAN ALES **/**
Dernière Volonté DIEU DU CIEL! **/ Hommel Bier** PERENNIAL ARTISAN ALES

ENGLISH BITTER ALE FISH AND CHIPS

ENGLISH BITTER

PICTURE A LOW-CEILINGED ROOM WITH DARK OAK BEAMS, A COZY TAVERN HUMMING WITH QUIET CONVERSATION, THE CRACKLE OF A FIREPLACE. You're in the Dove, Thameside, London. The bar itself is no bigger than a surfboard. On the walls of the humble alleyway tavern, said to be the oldest riverside bar in London (circa 1730), old photos display a history of illustrious clientele: writers Ernest Hemingway, Graham Greene, and Dylan Thomas, and the late patron saint of beer scribes, Michael Jackson, who lived nearby and came to the Dove often to drink his favorite pale ale, copper-hued Fuller's Chiswick Bitter. This is not a beer emporium; it's a beer sanctuary.

We ordinary people can still visit the Dove today, and when you get hungry, the gastropub-style kitchen delivers *perfect* fish and chips—sustainable haddock carefully breaded in local Fuller's London Pride beer.

Sounds nice, doesn't it? But if you can't make the trip soon, you can re-create part of the iconic atmosphere at home, with this recipe for traditional fish and chips. The trick to crispy, English-restaurant-quality chips at home is the double-fry: First you fry the potatoes at a relatively low temperature to draw out much of the moisture, then you raise the temperature of the oil and fry them again until crisp and golden brown. And for a simply brilliant beer to match, we love the now-classic Coniston Bluebird Bitter, exported to the best bottle shops around. Fuller's, of course, is also always a very nice beer with fish and chips.

Serves 4 to 6

4 LARGE RUSSET POTATOES, ABOUT 2 LB/910 G TOTAL WEIGHT

BEER BATTER
1½ CUPS/180 G ALL-PURPOSE FLOUR
1 TSP BAKING POWDER
1 TSP FINE SEA SALT
1½ CUPS/360 ML COLD ENGLISH BITTER ALE, PLUS MORE AS NEEDED

ABOUT 2 QT/2 L PEANUT OIL OR VEGETABLE OIL
FINE SEA SALT
1½ LB/680 G COD, POLLOCK, HADDOCK, HALIBUT, OR OTHER WHITE FLAKY FISH FILLETS, CUT INTO 4-IN/10-CM PIECES
¾ CUP/85 G CORNSTARCH
4 TO 6 FRESH PARSLEY SPRIGS
LEMON WEDGES, MALT VINEGAR, AND TARTAR SAUCE (RECIPE FOLLOWS) FOR SERVING

1. Peel the potatoes, but leave the skin intact on each end. Cut the potatoes lengthwise into ⅜-in/1-cm batons using a sharp chef's knife or a mandoline. Put the potatoes in a large bowl of cold water as you cut them. Refrigerate for at least 15 minutes, or up to 24 hours. Drain the potatoes and transfer to a clean kitchen towel. Blot very dry. Set aside for about 10 minutes to dry further.

2. TO MAKE THE BEER BATTER: Whisk together the flour, baking powder, and salt in a large bowl. Pour in the ale, whisking constantly to prevent lumps. Refrigerate the batter for at least 15 minutes, or up to 1 hour.

CONTINUED

3. Pour peanut oil into a large Dutch oven or other heavy-bottomed pot to a depth of 2 in/5 cm. Make sure there is at least 3 in/7.5 cm of space between the top of the oil and the top of the pot, to prevent boiling over when the potatoes are added (they cause the oil to bubble up quite a bit). Heat the oil over medium heat to 320°F/160°C. Have ready a baking sheet lined with paper towels.

4. Add the potatoes to the hot oil in handful-size batches. It's very important not to overcrowd the pot so that the chips fry evenly and the oil doesn't boil over. Fry until the edges are just starting to color, 2 to 3 minutes, adjusting the heat as needed to maintain the oil temperature. Transfer the chips to the prepared baking sheet to drain, using a slotted spoon or skimmer. Repeat to fry the remaining potatoes. Set the chips aside at room temperature.

5. Preheat the oven to 200°F/95°C, and set a wire rack on a large rimmed baking sheet to hold the finished chips. Raise the heat to bring the oil temperature to 375°F/190°C. Again working in batches, re-fry the potatoes until crisp and lightly browned, 2 to 4 minutes per batch. (Since much of the water has been drawn out during the first fry, you can now fry them in slightly larger batches without overflowing the oil.) Transfer the chips to the wire rack as they come out of the oil and sprinkle them generously with salt. When all of the chips are done, transfer the baking sheet to the oven to keep them warm while you fry the fish. Keep the oil at 375°F/190°C.

6. Set up another baking sheet lined with paper towels. Season the fish generously with salt. Stir the batter. (If it seems a little thick after resting, stir in another splash of beer. A slightly thinner batter yields a crisper crust, while a thicker batter yields a more doughy crust.) Put the cornstarch in a medium bowl. Toss a few of the fish pieces in the cornstarch to coat lightly and shake off the excess, then dip them in the batter to coat well. Slowly lower the coated fish pieces one at a time into the hot oil, still being careful not to overcrowd the pot. Fry, turning once or twice, until golden brown and crisp, 5 to 7 minutes. Transfer each batch of fried fish to the paper towels to drain as they are finished. Repeat to fry the remaining fillets. Transfer the baking sheet to the oven to keep warm with the chips. Keep the oil hot for the garnish.

7. Dip the parsley sprigs in the leftover batter and fry them in the hot oil until crisp, about 2 minutes.

8. Pile the chips on a large platter and top with the fried fish. Garnish with the fried parsley sprigs and the lemon wedges and serve immediately, with the malt vinegar and tartar sauce on the side.

OUR RECOMMENDED BREWS:

Bluebird Bitter CONISTON / **Bitter** RIDGEWAY / **Landlord Pale Ale** TIMOTHY TAYLOR / **Amerikaans** DE MOLEN / **London Pride** FULLER'S / **Bitter American** 21ST AMENDMENT / **Dale's Pale Ale** OSKAR BLUES

TARTAR SAUCE

Makes about 1 cup/240 ml

1 CUP/240 ML MAYONNAISE

½ CUP/10 G LOOSELY PACKED FRESH PARSLEY LEAVES

5 CORNICHONS OR 10 DILL PICKLE SLICES, COARSELY CHOPPED

2 TBSP CAPERS, DRAINED AND RINSED

1 TBSP FRESH LEMON JUICE

1 TSP SUGAR

½ TSP KOSHER SALT

PINCH OF FRESHLY GROUND PEPPER

DASH OF WORCESTERSHIRE SAUCE

DASH OF HOT-PEPPER SAUCE

Combine all of the ingredients in a food processor and pulse several times until the parsley, pickles, and capers are finely minced and the sauce is well blended but not puréed. Taste and adjust the seasoning. Refrigerate until chilled, at least 30 minutes or up to 3 days.

WOK-FIRED CHILE CRAB

AMERICAN-STYLE INDIA PALE ALE

BOTH OF US HAVE FAMILY TRADITIONS FOR EATING DUNGENESS CRAB ON SPECIAL OCCASIONS. Cracked casually onto a platter for hungry guests, these impressive creatures start an instant party. The question we ask ourselves: *Do I build a pile and risk a siege, or eat as I go, protecting every bite?*

However you devour it, crab has a remarkable power to elevate vibrant flavors, and in this flavorful East-meets-West dish, the heat of sambal chile paste; bright notes of ginger, garlic, cilantro, and green onion; and the umami in oyster sauce and soy sauce play off each other effortlessly. It makes a fantastically festive presentation. Be sure to offer moist hand towels or paper napkins and a bowl for the shells. Traditionally, this Singapore-inspired dish is served with rice or baguette; so consider that option, too, to make a meal. This is messy eating, but worth it.

And for the drinking part? You'll be doing plenty of that, trust us. With its spice, ocean airs, and power to ignite loud conversation (the good kind), chile crab begs for beer—big bottles of it. But while conventional wisdom would have you pairing this with light rice lager, mild hefeweizen, pale bock, and lighter saison, we recommend a tangy, potent, dry West Coast IPA, with juicy, citric hops that contrast the slightly sweet, miso-like flavor of the sauce; or even a double (a.k.a. Imperial) IPA, which amps up the alcohol, bitterness, mouthfeel, and fruitiness all around.

Serves 4

2 WHOLE COOKED DUNGENESS CRABS, ABOUT 4 LB/1.8 KG TOTAL WEIGHT

⅓ CUP/75 ML HEINZ CHILI SAUCE

2 TBSP OYSTER SAUCE

2 TBSP SOY SAUCE

1 TO 2 TBSP SAMBAL OELEK

1 TSP DISTILLED WHITE VINEGAR

1 TSP SUGAR

3 TBSP PEANUT OIL OR VEGETABLE OIL

4 GREEN ONIONS, WHITE AND GREEN PARTS, THINLY SLICED

ONE 1-IN/2.5-CM PIECE FRESH GINGER, PEELED AND FINELY CHOPPED

4 GARLIC CLOVES, FINELY CHOPPED

3 TBSP CHOPPED FRESH CILANTRO

1 LARGE EGG, BEATEN

1. Pull off the outer shells of the crabs and discard the spongy gills. Rinse the crabs under cold water to wash away the greenish-brown guts. Pull the legs from the bodies at their natural breaking point. Cut each body into quarters. Use a meat mallet or the spine of the knife to crack the legs and claws, keeping them mostly intact; set aside.

2. Stir together the chili sauce, oyster sauce, soy sauce, sambal oelek, vinegar, sugar, and ¼ cup/ 60 ml water in a medium bowl to make a stir-fry sauce. Set it near the stove.

3. Heat the peanut oil in a wok or a large sauté pan over high heat until you just begin to see wisps of smoke. Add about half of the green onions and all of the ginger and garlic and cook until softened and just beginning to brown, about 1 minute. Add the crab and toss it all together, about 1 minute. Pour in the sauce and stir-fry until the crab has absorbed most of the liquid, 6 to 8 minutes. Stir in 2 Tbsp of the cilantro and the egg and toss until the cilantro is evenly distributed and the egg is cooked into the sauce, about 1 minute longer.

4. Dump the crab into a large, wide serving dish and scrape out all the good stuff clinging to the pan. Garnish with the remaining green onions and cilantro and serve immediately, with a damp hand towel for each person instead of napkins.

OUR RECOMMENDED BREWS:

IPA STONE; PIKE BREWING CO.; SMUTTYNOSE / **Melrose IPA** BEACHWOOD BBQ / **Wipeout IPA** PORT BREWING

HOISIN-GLAZED PORK BELLY LETTUCE WRAPS
WITH PICKLED KUMQUATS, DAIKON, AND CARROTS

IMPERIAL IPA

IMPERIAL IPA, ALSO KNOWN AS DOUBLE IPA, IS, YOU COULD SAY, IPA ON STEROIDS. BUT DON'T WRITE IT OFF.
As an amped-up rendition of the American take on the original English style, IIPA/DIPA is characterized by massive malt and hop flavors that, in the wrong brewer's hands, pointlessly assail the tongue. In the right hands, however, it's a beer style with all the balance of IPA plus the heft of bigger beers, resulting in deliciously ripe, peachy, sometimes tropical flavors and aromas that are over the top and yet not, at the same time. Like IPA itself, this style was once at best an oddity and is now practically a standard in American breweries and taprooms.

To be sure, IIPA, while tantalizing, poses a brash challenge to food. But we found a great matchup: Pork belly, that culinary obsession of the late twentieth and early twenty-first century, has all the fattiness and flavor needed for the fight. If this popular but special cut of pork is not stocked regularly at your butcher's counter, just have them order it for you—the effort is worth it for this major party crowd-pleaser. In this fun, colorful dish, we found that the IIPA's citrus-smack and assertive bitterness make the pickled kumquats' flavor linger long after the first bite, while its malty backbone bear-hugs the fatty pork.

Serves 6 to 8

THE PICKLE

½ CUP/100 G SUGAR

⅜ CUP/90 ML RICE VINEGAR

1 TSP FINE SEA SALT

2 MEDIUM CARROTS, PEELED AND CUT INTO MATCHSTICKS

ONE 5-IN/12-CM DAIKON RADISH, PEELED AND CUT INTO MATCHSTICKS

12 KUMQUATS, THINLY SLICED AND SEEDED

2 LB/910 G SKINLESS PORK BELLY

1 HEAD GARLIC, CLOVES SEPARATED AND SMASHED BUT NOT PEELED

ONE 2-IN/5-CM PIECE FRESH GINGER, UNPEELED, CUT INTO COIN-SIZE SLICES

¼ CUP/60 ML SOY SAUCE, PLUS 3 TBSP

2 TSP FINE SEA SALT

ONE 22-OZ/650-ML BOTTLE PALE ALE

⅓ CUP/80 ML HOISIN SAUCE

2 TBSP SUGAR

1 OR 2 HEADS BUTTER LETTUCE, CORED AND SEPARATED INTO LEAVES

FRESH CILANTRO SPRIGS FOR GARNISH

SAMBAL OELEK OR SRIRACHA SAUCE FOR SERVING

1. **TO MAKE THE PICKLE:** Stir together the sugar, vinegar, salt, and 1 cup/240 ml water in a 1-qt/1-L glass jar or a medium bowl until the sugar dissolves. Add the carrots, daikon, and kumquats and push down gently to submerge. Cover and refrigerate for at least 2 hours, or up to 3 weeks.

2. Cut the pork belly against the grain into 20 slices about ½ in/12 mm thick and 5 in/12 cm long. Put the pork slices in a medium pot and add the garlic, ginger, ¼ cup/60 ml soy sauce, and salt. Pour in the ale, and then add enough water so that the pork is just barely covered. Bring to a boil over medium-high heat, then lower the heat to maintain a low simmer, cover, and cook until the pork is tender but still a little chewy, 35 to 40 minutes.

3. Position the broiler rack about 4 in/10 cm from the top heating element and preheat the broiler. Stir together the 3 Tbsp soy sauce, hoisin sauce, and sugar in a medium bowl and set aside.

4. Strain the pork belly from the broth and pat dry with paper towels. Discard the other solids and the broth. (Or, to save the broth for another use: Strain and let cool to room temperature. Refrigerate in a tightly covered container for up to 1 week or freeze for up to 1 year. Remove the solidified fat before using.) Toss the pork in the hoisin sauce mixture to coat evenly, and arrange the strips in a single layer on a rimmed baking sheet lined with aluminum foil. Broil the meat, turning once, until a charred crust forms on both sides, 3 to 4 minutes per side.

5. Select the sturdiest, cup-shaped lettuce leaves. Place each strip of pork in a lettuce-leaf cup and top with a pile of the pickle and a sprig of cilantro. Serve immediately, with the sambal oelek on the side.

OUR RECOMMENDED BREWS:

90-Minute IPA DOGFISH HEAD / **Heady Topper** THE ALCHEMIST / **Hopslam IPA** BELL'S BREWERY /
Wolf Among Weeds IPA GOLDEN ROAD / **Hoptimum** SIERRA NEVADA / **Pliny the Elder** RUSSIAN RIVER

MISO-MARINATED SHORT RIBS
WITH SHISHITO PEPPERS

BELGIAN PALE ALE

BREWED AT THE TRAPPIST ABBAYE NOTRE DAME D'ORVAL IN SOUTHERN BELGIUM, NEAR THE PROVINCE OF LUXEMBOURG, ORVAL IS AN ETHEREAL ALE SO DISTINCTIVE, SO INFLUENTIAL, AND SO ICONIC, THERE IS AT LEAST ONE AMERICAN BAR THAT WILL LITERALLY SERVE NO OTHER BREWS IN THE BOTTLE. A copper-hued, dry-finishing Belgian pale, Orval is the result of a circumspect "mixed fermentation" (using a blend of more than ten diverse yeast strains, including *Brettanomyces*), and its flavor has been the subject of admiration, curiosity, debate, and much imitation for decades.

Brewed since 1931 in the French-speaking Ardennes, between the serpentine Chiers and Semoy rivers, Orval now has a global following. What exactly makes this earthy, bright delicacy such an achievement is a long story, but for starters, Orval bursts with complex flavors of hay, orange peel, lemon, and leather. The first Trappist beer to be sold around Belgium, Orval snaps with the bite of three distinctive hops, and is bottle-conditioned, meaning it will change and improve over time if properly cellared. Even ten-year-old bottles can be crackling dry and improbably fresh and delicious.

Pairing Orval with food is easier said than done, but we found that the secret is umami, the "fifth taste" (see page 18). In this dish, umami—summoned by the mix of miso and meat—reigns supreme, and mighty Orval's flavors heighten its power.

Look for Korean-style beef short ribs, also called cross-cut flanken, or ask your butcher to cut them for you. This method cuts beef chuck ribs into thin strips across the bones, making them tender enough for quick-cooking techniques like grilling instead of requiring several hours of braising, as with conventional short ribs. With maximum surface area for picking up the marinade and developing a caramelized char, the resulting beef is deeply flavorful, with a pleasantly chewy texture. The grilled peppers and shichimi togarashi, a Japanese seven-spice chile powder mix, add a bit of fiery kick.

Serves 4 to 6

½ CUP/150 G RED MISO PASTE

½ CUP/120 ML MIRIN

½ CUP/120 ML PALE ALE

3 LB/1.4 KG KOREAN-STYLE OR FLANKEN BEEF SHORT RIBS, CUT ⅓ IN/8 MM THICK

ABOUT 1 LB/455 G SHISHITO PEPPERS

1 BUNCH GREEN ONIONS

PEANUT OIL OR VEGETABLE OIL FOR DRIZZLING

SHICHIMI TOGARASHI CHILE POWDER (SEE RECIPE INTRODUCTION) FOR SPRINKLING

1. Whisk together the miso, mirin, and ale in a small bowl. Pour the mixture into a large resealable plastic bag and add the short ribs. Seal the bag tightly, toss the meat around in the marinade to coat well, and refrigerate at least 4 hours, but preferably 8 hours or overnight.

2. Prepare a hot fire in a charcoal grill or preheat a gas grill to high. Soak several 8-in/20-cm wooden skewers in hot water for at least 30 minutes.

3. Trim any extra-long stems from the peppers. Trim the roots and any wilted tops from the green onions and cut them into pieces the same length as the peppers. Thread the peppers and green onions onto the soaked skewers, alternating the pieces. Drizzle the skewers lightly with peanut oil on a baking sheet and toss them around to coat.

4. Arrange the ribs on the hottest part of the grill rack and grill, turning once, until charred on the outside and still pink in the middle, about 3 minutes per side. Transfer to a platter and cover loosely with aluminum foil. Add the vegetable skewers to the grill and cook, turning as needed, until tender and lightly charred on both sides, 2 to 4 minutes per side.

5. Cut the ribs between each bone and pile them on a large platter. Arrange the vegetable skewers around the edges. Sprinkle it all with togarashi and serve immediately.

OUR RECOMMENDED BREWS:

Orval BRASSERIE D'ORVAL / **Rayon Vert** GREEN FLASH / **Sanctification** RUSSIAN RIVER / **Le Fleur Misseur** NEW BELGIUM BREWING / **It's Alive** MIKKELLER / **XH** HITACHINO NEST

Chapter 4
SOUR & COMPLEX

Of all the taste sensations, sour can seem the most exciting. Sourness, essentially acidity, awakens other senses, providing tantalizing counterpoints to salinity, spice, sweetness, and bitterness. It also brings on a powerful thirst. Sour beers comprise a range of styles emphasizing acidity over malt and hop flavors, and they're incredibly satisfying with the right foods.

Evidence suggests the first beers ever brewed on Earth—over eight thousand years ago—were unwittingly brewed with the help of sour-tasting wild yeast, though their makers thanked supernatural forces rather than *Lactobacillus*. One theory states that humans may have evolved to enjoy this bacterial tang because, as with other sour foods—kimchi and sauerkraut, for example—it encourages probiotic health.

Historically speaking, the beers famous for this flavor profile hail from Belgium (and, to a lesser extent, Germany). During the nineteenth century, advances in refrigeration, sanitation, beer transport, and especially yeast science led to the global boom in clear, golden, not-at-all-sour beer . . . but a few brewers, Belgians especially, held on. Belgian sour reds, browns, and lambics (spontaneously fermented ales, aged in French oak wine barrels for up to four years before being blended) are some of the most complex and engaging beers in the world, and the possibilities for pairing are endless.

Belgium nourished many other interesting beer traditions, including *saisons*, farmhouse ales brewed during cooler months for seasonal farmhands, or *saisonnierres*, to drink during harvest. These saison beers (or *seizoen*, in Flemish) are wonderfully complex, too, and traditionally have a pleasant, peppery bite and often a bit of wild, yeasty tang themselves. Straw-gold with a fluffy white head of foam, a good, grassy, herbal-tasting saison makes the perfect pairing to many a dish, especially cheeses. There are dark farmhouse ales, super-strong saisons, and farmhouse-inspired brews that have the added complexity of *Brettanomyces* yeast, with its phenolic, funky kick akin to tanned leather (which is probably why some craft beer cognoscenti call the taste and smell "horse blanket"!).

The arts of tart and farmhouse-style brewing have inspired countless innovations around the world. There are American wild ales and brilliantly sparkling Belgian blended lambics, called *gueuze*, that will send a bowl of steaming Mussels in Celery-Gueuze Cream (page 100) into the stratosphere. The best sweet-tart Flanders reds and browns, malty and tart, complement the Southeast Asian flavors of Tamarind Fish Sauce Wings (page 103) in ways we never expected. Sour beer lovers know what it can do with the right dish: light up taste buds in ways never expected. So pop a cork, pucker up, and prepare for some fireworks.

RACLETTE
WITH ROASTED ROOT VEGETABLES

SAISON

SAISON, THE FOOD-FRIENDLY CHAMELEON OF BEER STYLES (SEE PAGE 95), RANGES IN STRENGTH FROM AS LOW AS 4% ABV (WHEN IT IS SOMETIMES CALLED A GRISETTE) ALL THE WAY UP TO SOME 8 OR EVEN 9 PERCENT. Tropic King, from Fort Collins' Funkwerks brewery, is brewed with vibrant Rakau hops imported from New Zealand that impart peach- and mango-like flavors that make it a delicious, if perhaps surprising, match for gooey, aromatic alpine cheese served with simple roasted root vegetables.

This shared dish is a party theme in and of itself, yet surprisingly simple to prepare—after all, you're just broiling cheese. The secret is catching the perfect moment of viscosity, when the cheese is melted and oozy, but not separated and greasy. The sweetness of the roasted veggies plays a perfect counterpoint to the fruity, funky flavors of raclette, a raw cow's-milk cheese that's aged at least 5 months. As tradition dictates, you could also serve this festive, molten melted cheese with sliced cured meats like ham, prosciutto, and speck, for a more substantial offering.

Serves 6

2 LB/910 G MIXED ROOT VEGETABLES SUCH AS FINGERLING POTATOES, PARSNIPS, TURNIPS, RUTABAGAS, AND SUNCHOKES

3 TBSP EXTRA-VIRGIN OLIVE OIL

FINE SEA SALT

1 TSP SWEET PAPRIKA

1 LB/455 G RACLETTE CHEESE

CORNICHONS OR OTHER PICKLED VEGETABLES FOR SERVING

1. Position racks in the upper and lower thirds of the oven and preheat to 400°F/200°C.

2. Peel the larger root vegetables but leave the smaller ones with delicate skins (like fingerling potatoes) unpeeled. Cut the vegetables into slices or wedges that are all about ½ in/12 mm thick. Pile them on a large rimmed baking sheet. Drizzle with the olive oil, sprinkle with a big pinch of salt and the paprika, and toss to coat evenly. Spread in a single layer and roast on the top oven rack until tender, 20 to 25 minutes. While the vegetables are roasting, place a large cast-iron skillet on the bottom rack of the oven to heat.

3. Meanwhile, gently scrape the cheese rind with a knife to remove any film, but leave it intact. Cut the cheese into slices about ¼ in/6 mm thick.

4. When the vegetables are done, transfer to a serving platter. Turn the oven to broil. Add the cheese in a single layer to the hot skillet. Transfer the pan to the top oven rack (or the broiler drawer) and broil until the cheese is completely melted and just beginning to bubble at the edges, 3 to 4 minutes. Be careful not to overcook the cheese, or it will become greasy.

5. Serve the cheese immediately, directly from the skillet, with the roasted vegetables and cornichons and forks or metal skewers for dipping. If the cheese starts to solidify before it's all gone, slip it back under the broiler briefly to remelt.

OUR RECOMMENDED BREWS:

Tropic King FUNKWERKS / **Saison Dupont** BRASSERIE DUPONT / **Zaison** BREWERY VIVANT / **La Moneuse** BLAUGIES / **Zinnebir** BRASSERIE DE LA SENNE

SARDINES ON TOAST
WITH SHAVED FENNEL

SAISON

SAISON, OUR FAVORITE OVERALL FOOD-PAIRING STYLE, IS COMPOSED OF PILSNER AND WHEAT MALTS, AROMATIC HOPS, AND A PEPPERY YEAST STRAIN (OR THREE). The result is a worthy match for the unctuousness of sardines and their flavorsome counterparts here—piquant Pecorino cheese mixed with parsley leaves, crisp fennel, and a zingy lemony dressing.

With all of these flamboyant flavors, this beer style mingles confidently. Go with a stronger, potentially more funky or sour version (ideally, barrel-aged; a gueuze could also work, if you have access to one); lighter-flavored brews will drown. Like this dish, saisons are playful but serious in their own way. The slightly elevated booze levels advise a moderate pace, but add a certain something to the fresh ocean flavors of these beautiful diminutive fish.

Serves 6

1 LARGE FENNEL BULB, INCLUDING FRONDS

1 CUP/20 G LOOSELY PACKED FRESH PARSLEY LEAVES

1½ OZ/40 G PECORINO ROMANO CHEESE, CUT INTO TINY CUBES

2 TBSP CAPERS, DRAINED AND RINSED

FINE SEA SALT AND FRESHLY GROUND PEPPER

½ LEMON

EXTRA-VIRGIN OLIVE OIL FOR DRIZZLING AND BRUSHING

6 LARGE OR 12 SMALL FRESH SARDINES, ABOUT 2 LB/910 G TOTAL WEIGHT, CLEANED, SPLIT, AND BONED, OR THREE 4-OZ/115-G CANS SARDINES PACKED IN WATER OR OLIVE OIL, DRAINED

6 LARGE SLICES COUNTRY BREAD

1. Trim and discard the green stalk from the fennel bulb, reserving some frond sprigs for garnish. Trim the root end and cut the fennel bulb in half lengthwise. Carve out the triangular core from each half, then very thinly slice the fennel using a mandoline or a sharp chef's knife.

2. Toss the fennel with the parsley, pecorino, capers, and a pinch of salt and pepper in a large bowl. Squeeze in the juice from the lemon half, drizzle lightly with olive oil, and toss it all together. Taste and adjust the seasoning.

3. Pat the sardines dry with paper towels. Brush them with olive oil and season both sides with salt and pepper. Drizzle the bread slices generously with oil, too. Heat a cast-iron skillet or grill pan over high heat. Grill the bread until nicely charred on both sides, about 2 minutes per side; set aside. Put the sardines in the pan, skin-side down, and sear until lightly charred, about 1 minute. Turn carefully and cook until seared on the second side and cooked through, about 1 minute longer. (If using canned sardines, just grill the bread and skip to the next step to assemble.)

4. Place a sardine (or two, if you used smaller or canned fish), skin-side up, on each piece of toasted bread and top with a pile of the salad. Drizzle with a little more oil, mound a small handful of the reserved fennel fronds on each, and serve immediately.

OUR RECOMMENDED BREWS:

Tank 7 BOULEVARD / Love Buzz Saison ANCHORAGE / Saison Renaud MYSTIC / HandFarm TIRED HANDS BREWING COMPANY / Red Barn LOST ABBEY / Xxtra THIRIEZ

SHIITAKE GYOZAS
WITH PLUM VINEGAR

BLACK FARMHOUSE ALE

COMPLEX, FOOD-FRIENDLY FARMHOUSE ALES FROM BELGIUM AND NORTHERN FRANCE, ONCE OBSCURE, HAVE FUELED A GLOBAL RENAISSANCE OF EXPERIMENTATION AND IMPROVISATION. And while it's debatable whether or not an operation lacking farmland, livestock, or a tractor can truly call itself a "farmhouse brewery," it's beyond question that this genre of spicy, many-layered beers is a great companion to cuisines from around the globe.

Farmhouse ales are by turns fruity, spicy, complex, dry, hazy; occasionally dark or strong; and always interesting. With a base usually including barley, wheat (unmalted and sometimes acidulated), spicy noble hops, fragrant peppery yeasts, and sometimes herbs, they are to Belgium what IPA is to England: an export that has inspired and fueled and expanded the global craft-beer revolution.

Umeboshi plum vinegar—made from a pickled Japanese fruit referred to as a plum but closer to an apricot—has been available, although obscure, since the 1970s, when interest in Japanese cuisine and macrobiotic foods began to expand in the United States. Look for it in specialty-foods markets and Asian groceries. In this dish, the umami (see page 18) of the earthy mushrooms and salty, funky umeboshi do a complex dance, but the right dark or black farmhouse ale takes its hand. The earthy, roasted, umami- and faintly soy sauce–esque flavors of dark malt waltz with the shiitake, while the caramelized edges of the dumpling wrappers, the spicy hops, and the tang of wild yeasts all fall into step with the vinegar itself. Black saison and dark farmhouse ales aren't always easy to find, but they're worth extra effort.

Makes 40 dumplings

4 CUPS/360 G FINELY SHREDDED NAPA CABBAGE

1 TSP FINE SEA SALT

ABOUT 6 TSP SESAME OIL

2 GREEN ONIONS, WHITE AND GREEN PARTS, THINLY SLICED

2 LARGE GARLIC CLOVES, FINELY MINCED

1 TSP PEELED AND GRATED FRESH GINGER

10 OZ/280 G SHIITAKE MUSHROOMS, BRUSHED CLEAN AND FINELY CHOPPED

2 TBSP WHITE MISO PASTE

4 TBSP/60 ML UMEBOSHI PLUM VINEGAR

1 LARGE EGG

40 ROUND GYOZA OR POTSTICKER WRAPPERS

CHILI OIL OR HOT SESAME OIL FOR SERVING

1. Put the cabbage in a medium bowl and sprinkle with the salt. Gently massage the salt into the cabbage, using your hands. Set aside for about 15 minutes to allow the salt to extract some of the water from the cabbage and tenderize it. Wrap the cabbage in a clean kitchen towel or cheesecloth and squeeze out as much water as possible. Set aside.

2. Heat 3 tsp of the sesame oil in a large skillet over medium-high heat. Add the green onions, garlic, and ginger and stir-fry until softened and aromatic, about 30 seconds. Add the mushrooms and stir-fry until they release their liquid and it evaporates, 6 to 8 minutes. Remove the pan from the heat and let the mushroom mixture cool to room temperature.

3. Whisk together the miso, 1 Tbsp of the vinegar, and the egg in a large bowl. Add the mushroom mixture and the cabbage and mix and mash everything together to make a cohesive, compact filling (this will make it easier to enclose in the wrappers).

4. Have a small bowl of cold water nearby. Lay a gyoza wrapper on a clean work surface. Place a scant 1 Tbsp of the filling in the center of the wrapper. Dip a fingertip in the cold water and moisten the edges of the wrapper. Fold the edges of the wrapper together to enclose the filling and create a half-circle dumpling. Pinch the edges together tightly to seal. Pleat the edge by folding it back onto itself every ¼ in/6 mm or so; you'll make about five pleats in all. Set the finished gyoza on a baking sheet with the pleated edge up. Repeat to make a total of 40 gyozas.

5. Heat 1 tsp of the remaining sesame oil in a large, nonstick skillet over medium-high heat. Have ready a lid that fits the skillet. Add as many of the gyozas, pleats pointed up, as will fit in the skillet without touching each other and cook until deeply browned and crusty on the bottom, about 2 minutes. Using the lid to shield yourself from spatter, pour in ¼ cup/ 60 ml water and quickly cover the pan with the lid to trap the steam (and the spatter). Immediately turn the heat to medium-low and steam the gyozas until the wrappers are translucent and glossy, 2 to 3 minutes. Remove the lid and raise the heat to medium. Continue cooking until the water evaporates and only the oil remains, shaking the skillet occasionally to be sure the gyozas aren't sticking, 1 to 2 minutes longer. Transfer the gyozas to a serving platter. Wipe out the skillet with a paper towel and repeat to cook the rest.

6. Stir together the remaining 3 Tbsp vinegar and a few dashes of chili oil in a small bowl and place it on the serving platter. Serve immediately.

OUR RECOMMENDED BREWS:

Black Metal JESTER KING / **Humulus Nocta** FLAT TAIL / **Edith** HILL FARMSTEAD / **Existent** STILLWATER / **Aberrance** JACKIE O'S

MUSSELS IN CELERY-GUEUZE CREAM

GUEUZE

FIRST OF ALL, GUEUZE, A COPPER-HUED BLEND OF YOUNG AND AGED LAMBIC, THE FAMOUS SPONTANEOUSLY FERMENTED BELGIAN ALE, IS PRONOUNCED SOMEWHERE ALONG THE LINES OF "GHERZ" AND "GOOZE" (GO AHEAD, GIVE IT A TRY). Lemon-tart, musty, and minerally, with carbonation derived from the same process as Champagne, it's one of the world's most remarkable beer styles, and is astonishingly good with certain foods.

Once the most popular style in Brussels, gueuze is the product of ultra-traditional breweries that very nearly disappeared completely in the 1960s. The war, and a century of rationalization and closures—and shifting popular tastes—had made gueuze seem an oddity instead of the vibrant, incredible beverage it really is. Desperate, area brewers started adding artificial sweeteners in a misguided plea for popular taste, which made the beers, well, disgustingly ordinary.

Fortunately, there was one very, very important holdout. Jean Pierre Van Roy, of Brasserie Cantillon, founded in the Anderlecht neighborhood of Brussels in 1900, persisted in making uncompromising lambics according to the old, unsweetened ways, turning his little family brewery into a Brussels tourist attraction (Le Musée Bruxellois de la Gueuze) and expanding his family, which still runs the brewery together, led by his affable son Jean.

And what to eat with a great gueuze like Cantillon's? A bowl of steaming mussels is one of the most appetizing, satisfying dishes imaginable, smelling of the sea and aromatic herbs and vegetables, and the joy of the crusty bread you must have at the ready for dipping. It's also the national dish of Belgium, available . . . everywhere. The acidity of the beer really pops in the broth, and the faint bitterness—very faint—works in tandem with the mineral notes of the mussels and the fragrance of celery and thyme. The beer's tight, light carbonation has a mouth-cleansing aspect, and overall the effect is, like Cantillon, magical.

Serves 4 to 6

4 TBSP/55 G UNSALTED BUTTER

4 CELERY STALKS, THINLY SLICED ON THE DIAGONAL

2 LARGE SHALLOTS, THINLY SLICED

4 GARLIC CLOVES, THINLY SLICED

4 FRESH THYME SPRIGS

½ TSP FRESHLY GROUND WHITE PEPPER

1 CUP/240 ML GUEUZE BEER

½ CUP/120 ML HEAVY CREAM

FINE SEA SALT

2 LB/910 G PRINCE EDWARD ISLAND MUSSELS, SCRUBBED WELL AND DEBEARDED

3 TBSP COARSELY CHOPPED FRESH PARSLEY

ARTISAN FRENCH BREAD FOR SERVING

CONTINUED

1. Melt the butter over medium-low heat in a large Dutch oven. When the foam subsides, add the celery, shallots, garlic, thyme, and pepper and cook, stirring occasionally, until the vegetables are soft but not brown, about 5 minutes.

2. Add the beer, cream, and a big pinch of salt. Raise the heat to high to bring the mixture to a boil. Add the mussels to the pot and toss to coat them in the broth. Cover the pot tightly and steam until the mussels open, about 3 minutes. Remove the lid and stir in the parsley. (Discard any mussels that fail to open.)

3. Taste the broth and adjust the seasoning. Serve the mussels directly from the pot at the table, ladling a good amount of broth into each bowl. Pass plenty of bread for dipping.

OUR RECOMMENDED BREWS:

Oude Gueuze CANTILLON / **Golden Blend** DRIE FONTEINEN / **à l'Ancienne** GUEUZERIE TILQUIN / **Oude Gueuze** DE CAM / **Gueuze** GIRARDIN / **Coolship Resurgam** ALLAGASH

TAMARIND-FISH SAUCE WINGS

FLANDERS RED

OUR TAMARIND-SPIKED WINGS—INSPIRED BY THE FAMOUS PORTLAND, OREGON, RESTAURANT POK POK'S VIETNAMESE FISH SAUCE WINGS—BURST WITH SWEET-SOUR SOUTHEAST ASIAN FLAVORS OF FUNKY FISH SAUCE, TAMARIND, FIERY SPICE, AND GARLIC THAT CRY OUT FOR A ROBUST BEER. While conventional wisdom dictates an icy, brewed-in-Thailand Singha or some other pale international lager as the go-to, we found that one of the world's great styles, Flanders red out of Belgium, inspired a much more fun, flavorful, sweet-sour surprise. Traditionally fermented for extended periods (6 to 36 months!) in huge oak vats called *foeders,* and later re-fermented with younger beer, Flanders red is distinguished by its garnet color, complex tart-sweet palate, and clean finish, all of which make it work surprisingly well with these wings. Its acidity accentuates the tart fruitiness of tamarind pulp, while the funky yeast profile echoes the pungency of fish sauce. Best of all, it's typically light enough (traditionally around 5 to 7% ABV) to be refreshing throughout a long session.

Serves 4

6 GARLIC CLOVES, FINELY MINCED
½ CUP/120 ML VIETNAMESE FISH SAUCE
½ CUP/100 G SUGAR
2 LB/910 G CHICKEN WINGS, CUT AT THE JOINTS
1 TBSP SEEDLESS TAMARIND PULP (SEE NOTE ON PAGE 43)
PEANUT OIL OR VEGETABLE OIL FOR FRYING
1 CUP/100 G RICE FLOUR
2 TSP RED PEPPER FLAKES
2 TBSP COARSELY CHOPPED FRESH CILANTRO
2 TBSP SLICED GREEN ONIONS, WHITE AND GREEN PARTS

1. Put the garlic in a small, heatproof bowl and pour in ¼ cup/60 ml hot water; let sit for about 5 minutes. Drain the garlic in a fine-mesh sieve set over a bowl. Using the back of a spoon, press the garlic against the sieve to remove as much water as possible. Transfer the garlic to a small bowl and reserve.

2. Add the fish sauce and sugar to the bowl of garlic water and whisk until the sugar dissolves. Put the chicken wings in a large resealable plastic bag. Add ½ cup/120 ml of the fish sauce mixture, seal the bag tightly, and toss the chicken around to coat in the marinade. Let the wings marinate in the refrigerator for at least 4 hours, or preferably overnight, tossing the bag every so often.

CONTINUED

3. Meanwhile, combine the tamarind pulp and ¼ cup/ 60 ml water in a small saucepan and bring to a boil. Remove from the heat and break up the pulp with a wooden spoon, then cover and set aside to soften, about 10 minutes. Mash up the softened tamarind pulp to dissolve. Pour the mixture through a fine-mesh sieve into the fish sauce mixture remaining in the bowl. Use the back of the wooden spoon to aggressively mash and push as much of the pulp through as possible; discard the solids. Keep the tamarind–fish sauce mixture in the refrigerator, covered, until ready to use.

4. Next, pour peanut oil into a small saucepan to a depth of ½ in/12 mm and heat over high heat. Set a fine-mesh sieve in a medium bowl and place it near the stove. To test if the oil is hot enough, drop in a piece of the garlic; it should sizzle enthusiastically on contact. When the oil is hot, add all of the garlic at once. Turn the heat to medium-low and fry, stirring occasionally, until the garlic is light golden brown, 3 to 5 minutes. Drain the garlic in the sieve, then transfer to paper towels to drain further and cool. Set aside. (You can store the fried garlic, covered in the refrigerator, for up to 24 hours. Keep the garlic-infused oil in the refrigerator for another use, like stir-frying, if you like.)

5. When you are ready to fry the wings, drain them in a colander set in the sink. Pour peanut oil into a wok or large pot to a depth of 1 in/2.5 cm and heat it over medium-high heat until a deep-fry thermometer registers 325°F/165°C. Meanwhile, line a large baking sheet with paper towels and set it near the stove.

6. While the oil is heating, put the rice flour in a large bowl and toss the wings in it to coat evenly. Shake off any excess flour and add half of the wings to the hot oil. Fry until golden brown and crisp, 10 to 12 minutes, turning with tongs every few minutes and adjusting the heat as needed to maintain the oil temperature. Transfer the wings to the prepared baking sheet to drain. Allow the heat to return to 325°F/165°C, then fry the rest of the wings the same way.

7. Bring half of the tamarind–fish sauce mixture to a full boil in a nonstick wok or sauté pan over medium-high heat and cook until slightly thickened, about 30 seconds. Add half of the wings and toss to coat. Turn the heat to medium and continue cooking and tossing the wings until a caramelized glaze coats them evenly, about 1 minute. Sprinkle half of the fried garlic and 1 tsp of the red pepper flakes evenly over the wings and toss well. Transfer to a serving platter and sprinkle with half of the cilantro and green onions. Wipe out the wok with paper towels and repeat to fry the remaining batch. Serve immediately.

SAVOY CABBAGE ROLLS
WITH BEEF AND BARLEY AND ALE CREAM

SAISON

THANKS TO THE PRESENCE OF WILD YEASTS AND STRONG LACTIC STRAINS, FARMHOUSE ALES USED TO BE RATHER SOUR, AND AROUND THE WORLD, MANY BREWERS HAVE BEEN EXPERIMENTING WITH BRINGING THOSE ACIDIC ANGLES BACK—FOR STARTERS, BECAUSE THEY ARE EVEN MORE INTRIGUING AND DELICIOUS WITH FOOD.

One of the most innovative brewers of Old World saisons is The Commons, in Southeast Portland, Oregon, which opened in 2012. There, founder Mike Wright and brewmaster Sean Burke have fostered a culture of quiet excellence, with world-class Belgian-style beers that have already racked up plenty of medals and attention from aficionados.

Of all the beers they've released, Myrtle is one of the most interesting, ideal with Northern European food like this decidedly fancified take on cabbage rolls. Cloaked in lacy savoy cabbage, the savory beef-and-barley melange is accented by a delicate cream sauce made with the complex ale. Together, the beer's lemony tartness sets up interesting contrasts that really bring out the dish's barley flavor.

Serves 6 to 12

3 CUPS/720 ML GOOD-QUALITY LOW-SODIUM BEEF OR VEGETABLE STOCK

1 CUP/185 G HULLED BARLEY

FINE SEA SALT

1 LARGE HEAD SAVOY CABBAGE

2 TBSP EXTRA-VIRGIN OLIVE OIL

1 MEDIUM YELLOW ONION, FINELY DICED

2 LARGE GARLIC CLOVES, MINCED

2 TBSP FINELY CHOPPED FRESH THYME

2 TSP CARAWAY SEEDS, LIGHTLY CRUSHED IN A MORTAR WITH A PESTLE OR IN A SPICE GRINDER

½ TSP FRESHLY GROUND PEPPER

1 LB/455 G GROUND BEEF

½ CUP/120 ML SOUR CREAM

2 LARGE EGGS, LIGHTLY BEATEN

2 CUPS/480 ML SAISON

2 TBSP JUNIPER BERRIES

1. Combine the beef stock and barley in a small saucepan and bring to a boil over high heat. Lower the heat to maintain a low simmer, cover, and cook until the barley is tender but still chewy and just about all the liquid has been absorbed, 45 minutes to 1 hour. Season with salt and set aside to cool.

2. Preheat the oven to 375°F/190°C.

3. Bring a large pot of water to a boil over high heat and season it well with salt. Trim the core from the cabbage and carefully peel apart the leaves to get 12 large, sturdy leaves to stuff. (Discard the outer leaves if they are bruised or wilted, and reserve the remaining cabbage for another use.) Add the cabbage leaves to the boiling water and cook until bright green and just tender, 5 to 7 minutes. Drain in a colander, then lay them out on kitchen towels to cool and dry.

4. Meanwhile, heat the olive oil in a sauté pan over medium heat. Add the onion and sauté until tender and lightly browned, 5 to 7 minutes. Stir in the garlic, thyme, caraway seeds, and pepper and cook until aromatic, about 1 minute longer. Scrape the onion mixture into a large bowl and set aside to cool a few minutes.

5. Add the barley, beef, ¼ cup/60 ml of the sour cream, the eggs, and 2 tsp salt to the onion mixture. Stir and squish everything together with your hands until the filling is well blended and has a uniform consistency.

6. Arrange the cabbage leaves on a clean work surface with the cupped side facing up. Divide the filling evenly among the leaves. Beginning with the stem end, fold each cabbage leaf over the filling, overlapping them in the center to make roundish stuffed cabbage patties.

7. Carefully place the cabbage rolls, seam-side down, in a single layer in a 13-by-9-in/33-by-23-cm baking dish; they should fit snugly. Pour in the saison, sprinkle the juniper berries around pockets in the bottom of the dish, and cover tightly with aluminum foil. Bake for 25 minutes, then remove the foil and continue baking the cabbage rolls, uncovered, until the tops are very lightly colored, about 15 minutes longer.

8. Transfer the cabbage rolls to a platter. Strain the pan juices into a medium saucepan and bring to a boil over high heat. Whisk in the remaining ¼ cup/60 ml sour cream and season with salt. Spoon the sauce over the cabbage rolls and serve immediately.

OUR RECOMMENDED BREWS:

Myrtle THE COMMONS BREWERY / **Vieille** CROOKED STAVE / **Arctic Saison** GRASSROOTS / **Anna** HILL FARMSTEAD / **Bam Bière** JOLLY PUMPKIN

MEATBALLS MARRAKESH

BIÈRE DE MARS

FRANCE HAS NEVER BEEN KNOWN FOR ITS BEER TRADITIONS, BUT SLOWLY, THINGS ARE CHANGING.

One reason is the revival of bière de garde, a top-fermented brew from the Nord-Pas de Calais region of France, known as the "French Flanders." Similar to Belgium's saison, bière de garde comes in many variations, such as bière de Mars, a limited-release version brewed in March and sometimes given some added complexity with barrel aging. Beyond its timing, there's little to define a bière de Mars, but some American versions accentuate the earthy, "barnyardy" flavors of *Brettanomyces* yeast.

Kefta, heavily spiced Moroccan meatballs, are served on skewers from roadside food stands throughout the country, and are found braised in fragrant sauces in tagines. This home version is the perfect hot appetizer for a large party because they hold up well in a chafing dish or slow cooker, permeating the room with an exotic fragrance, for hours. In this dish, olives, full-flavored red meats, tomatoes, and Moroccan spices combine deliciously for super-savory bites. As a table beer should, the versatile bière de Mars matches those flavor components well, without overwhelming the dish or running from it.

Serves 4 to 6

1½ LB/680 G GROUND LAMB OR BEEF, PREFERABLY A MIXTURE OF BOTH

1 LARGE YELLOW ONION, FINELY CHOPPED

3 GARLIC CLOVES, MINCED

3 TBSP FINELY MINCED FRESH PARSLEY

1 TSP FINE SEA SALT

1 TSP GROUND CORIANDER

½ TSP GROUND CUMIN

¼ TSP CAYENNE PEPPER

ALL-PURPOSE FLOUR FOR DUSTING

1 DRIED RED CHILE SUCH AS ANCHO OR NEW MEXICO

2 TBSP EXTRA-VIRGIN OLIVE OIL, PLUS MORE AS NEEDED

1 LB/455 G RIPE TOMATOES, PEELED, SEEDED, AND FINELY CHOPPED (JUICE RESERVED), OR ONE 14½-OZ/415-G CAN DICED TOMATOES, WITH JUICE

1 TSP GROUND CINNAMON

½ TSP SWEET PAPRIKA

8 OZ/230 G PITTED BLACK OLIVES SUCH AS KALAMATA OR GAETA

WARM PITA BREAD, CUT INTO WEDGES, FOR SERVING

1. Combine the ground meat, about half of the onion, the garlic, parsley, salt, ground coriander, cumin, and cayenne in a large bowl. Using your hands, knead everything together until it binds, but not so long that it becomes completely homogenous and pastelike. You should still be able to distinguish bits of ground meat. With slightly wet hands, form the meat mixture into small meatballs, each about 1½ in/ 4 cm in diameter.

CONTINUED

2. Pour flour into a shallow bowl or onto a work surface. Roll the meatballs in the flour to coat lightly. Set aside at room temperature for 30 minutes to 1 hour to allow the flavors to meld.

3. Meanwhile, stem and halve the dried chile, remove the seeds, and chop it into small pieces. Put the chopped chile in a small, heatproof bowl and pour in ¼ cup/60 ml hot water. Soak until softened, 30 minutes to 1 hour.

4. Heat the olive oil in a large Dutch oven or other heavy-bottomed pot with a tight-fitting lid over medium heat. Add the meatballs and cook, turning as needed, until evenly browned on all sides, 8 to 10 minutes total. Transfer the meatballs to a plate using a slotted spoon and set aside. Add the remaining onion to the same oil, turn the heat to medium-low, and cook until soft and translucent, about 5 minutes. Add the tomatoes with their juice, rehydrated chile and soaking water, cinnamon, paprika, and about ½ cup/120 ml water and bring to a boil over medium-high heat, stirring. Return the meatballs to the pot, along with any juices accumulated on the plate. Add the olives and lower the heat to maintain a low simmer. Cover partially and simmer until the sauce thickens slightly, the flavors meld, and the meatballs are cooked through, about 30 minutes. (At this point, the meatballs can be cooled to room temperature and refrigerated in an airtight container for up to 5 days or frozen for up to 3 months. Reheat before serving.)

5. Taste and adjust the seasoning. Serve hot, in a chafing dish, slow cooker, or directly from the Dutch oven, with pita wedges on the side.

OUR RECOMMENDED BREWS:

Bière de Mars JOLLY PUMPKIN **/ La Bavaisienne** THEILLIER **/ Les Sans Culottes** LA CHOULETTE **/ Bière de Mars, Lips of Faith Series** NEW BELGIUM BREWING **/ Abbaye de Saint Bon-Chien** BRASSERIE DES FRANCHES-MONTAGNES

KRIEK-BRAISED PORK SLIDERS

KRIEK

TRADITIONAL KRIEK IS BELGIAN LAMBIC (SPONTANEOUS OR WILD ALE; SEE PAGE 100), BLENDED WITH REAL CHERRIES, AND IT'S A DELICACY TO BE SAVORED. After all, it takes a good 18 to 36 months to make one batch, carefully barrel-aged to perfection and then blended with younger beer.

It's also absolutely delicious with the right foods. (Avoid versions with artificial cherry flavor; those chemical flavors will ruin the patient work within your bottle.) In this massively satisfying preparation, a good kriek's tartness and acidity tenderize and flavor your pork shoulder to falling-apart perfection. Pair one or more tart krieks with each bite and compare the results.

Serves 6 to 8

1 BONELESS PORK SHOULDER, 2 TO 2½ LB/ 910 G TO 1.2 KG, TRIMMED OF EXCESS FAT

FINE SEA SALT AND FRESHLY GROUND PEPPER

3 SLICES SMOKED BACON, DICED

1 LARGE YELLOW ONION, DICED

4 LARGE GARLIC CLOVES, MINCED

ONE 22-OZ/650-ML BOTTLE KRIEK

½ CUP/80 G DRIED CHERRIES, COARSELY CHOPPED

¼ CUP/75 G CHERRY JAM OR RED CURRANT JELLY

16 SLIDER BUNS OR DINNER ROLLS, HALVED

1. Preheat the oven to 325°F/165°C. Pat the pork dry with paper towels, then sprinkle it generously with salt and pepper. Set aside to allow to come to room temperature.

2. Heat a Dutch oven or other heavy-bottomed, ovenproof pot with a tight-fitting lid over medium heat. Add the bacon and sauté until crisp but still a little chewy, about 5 minutes. Transfer the bacon to a plate using a slotted spoon. Raise the heat to high and add the pork to the pan, fat-side down. Sear to get a nice brown crust on all sides, turning as needed, about 10 minutes total. Transfer the pork to a plate.

3. Turn the heat to medium and add the onion to the same pot. Sauté until lightly browned, about 5 minutes. Add the garlic and cook for 1 minute. Stir in the kriek, scraping the browned bits from the bottom and sides of the pot. Return the pork and bacon to the pot. Raise the heat to high and bring to a boil, then cover and transfer the pot to the oven to braise until the meat is falling-apart tender, 2½ to 3 hours.

4. Remove the pork from the pot. Skim the excess fat from the surface of the braising liquid, if needed. Stir in the cherries and jam and bring the liquid to a boil over high heat. Cook until it reduces to a saucy consistency, 5 to 7 minutes. While the sauce reduces, use two forks to shred the meat. Stir the meat back into the pot to coat in the thickened sauce. Taste and adjust the seasoning. (The pulled pork can be made up to 5 days ahead. Let cool to room temperature, then cover tightly and refrigerate. Rewarm gently in a saucepan or the oven before serving.)

5. Pile the hot pulled pork between the slider buns, dividing it evenly. Serve immediately.

OUR RECOMMENDED BREWS:

Cerasus LOGSDON FARMHOUSE ALES / The Dissident DESCHUTES BREWERY / Dogpatch Sour ALMANAC / Kriek DE RANKE / Kriek Mariage Parfait BOON

CIVILIZED STEAK SANDWICHES
WITH GENTLEMAN'S RELISH

FLANDERS RED

WHAT COULD BE MORE CIVILIZED THAN A PERFECT STEAK SANDWICH? A rich steak sandwich served with a nice Flanders red, aged, tart-sweet, and woody, that's what. West Flanders was once part of Burgundy, and, today, Belgians use an expression to refer to lovers of food and drink as Burgundians. So it's not a stretch at all to say that beer truly is the Burgundy of Belgium, and Flemish red, also known as Flanders red, is one of the country's most beloved styles, not to be confused with Flanders brown, or Oud Bruin, which hails from East Flanders.

It can be shocking, to the uninitiated, to taste one of these tart, winelike Flanders reds for the first time. Flavors akin to plum, wood, vinegar, cola, raisin, and red fruits like cherry and raspberry abound. The beers have almost no hop character, but some fine tannic qualities, and a moderate alcohol range of 6 to 8% ABV. Thanks to their bracing acidity, Flanders reds can be great with food, possessing both the angularity and depth of flavor required by fatty meats and sauces.

As for this highly esteemed sandwich, the key to its success is twofold. First, the bread: search out a loaf with a relatively tender crust that isn't too chewy, or it will be hard to eat while everything slides out the sandwich on the other end. Meanwhile, the Gentleman's Relish, a delicacy born in 1828 out of Victorian and Edwardian English tastes, is traditionally spread on toast with cucumber, but it's also delicious served as a dollop on a freshly grilled, medium-rare steak; the combination, naturally, is twice as civilized.

Serves 6 to 12

GENTLEMAN'S RELISH

10 TBSP/140 G UNSALTED BUTTER, AT ROOM TEMPERATURE

¼ TSP CAYENNE PEPPER

¼ TSP GROUND GINGER

¼ TSP FRESHLY GROUND BLACK PEPPER

⅛ TSP GROUND CINNAMON

PINCH OF GROUND MACE OR NUTMEG

TWO 2-OZ/56-G TINS OIL-PACKED ANCHOVIES, DRAINED

2 THICK-CUT BONELESS NEW YORK STRIP STEAKS, ABOUT 12 OZ/340 G EACH

FINE SEA SALT AND COARSELY GROUND BLACK PEPPER

1½ TBSP OLIVE OIL, PLUS MORE FOR DRIZZLING

1 LARGE SWEET YELLOW ONION, CUT INTO ¾-IN/2-CM DICE

1 LARGE CIABATTA LOAF

1 SMALL CUCUMBER, SCRUBBED BUT NOT PEELED, THINLY SLICED INTO ROUNDS

1 BUNCH WATERCRESS, TRIMMED TO INCLUDE 2 IN/5 CM OF STEM ATTACHED TO THE LEAVES, OR 3 BIG HANDFULS BABY ARUGULA

1. **TO MAKE THE RELISH:** Melt 2 Tbsp of the butter in a small saucepan over medium-low heat. When it begins to sizzle, stir in the cayenne, ginger, black pepper, cinnamon, and mace. Cook, stirring constantly, until the spices are aromatic, about 30 seconds. Remove the pan from the heat and scrape the contents into a food processor. Add the remaining 8 Tbsp/115 g butter and the anchovies and process to a smooth paste. Transfer the relish to a small bowl or glass jar, cover, and refrigerate until set, at least 30 minutes. (The relish will keep, covered in the refrigerator, for up to 1 week.)

2. Season the steaks generously with salt and black pepper on both sides and set aside for about 1 hour to let come to room temperature. Heat the olive oil in a large cast-iron skillet or sauté pan over high heat until you just begin to see wisps of smoke. Add the steaks and sear on each side until a deep-brown crust forms, 1½ to 2 minutes per side. Turn the heat to low and cook the steaks, turning once, until an instant-read thermometer inserted into the thickest part of the meat registers 120°F/48°C for medium-rare, 5 to 8 minutes total. Transfer the steaks to a cutting board and cover with aluminum foil to rest for at least 10 minutes. Carve the steaks against the grain on the diagonal into very thin slices.

3. Return the pan to medium heat and add a drizzle of olive oil. Add the onion and a big pinch of salt and sauté until the onion is tender and nicely charred at the edges, 6 to 8 minutes. Turn the heat to medium-low if it begins to burn.

4. Preheat the broiler. Cut the ciabatta in half horizontally so that there is a top and a bottom and place the halves, cut-side up, on a large baking sheet. Broil until toasted, 1 to 2 minutes.

5. Spread both sides of the bread with a good smear of the relish. On the top half, place the cucumber slices in an overlapping layer. On the bottom half, layer the steak, then the onion. Mound the watercress over the onion and cover with the top half of the bread. Place 6-in/15-cm wooden skewers in the sandwich every 2 in/5 cm or so, to hold the sandwiches together after they are cut. Slice the sandwich with a serrated knife between the skewers and serve immediately, on a long wooden cutting board or large platter.

OUR RECOMMENDED BREWS:

Grand Cru RODENBACH / **Duchesse de Bourgogne** VERHAEGHE / **Panil Barriqueé Sour** BIRRIFICIO TORRECHIARA / **Dogpatch Sour** ALMANAC / **Cuvée des Jacobins Rouge** BOCKOR

CARBONADE HAND PIES

OUD BRUIN/FLANDERS BROWN ALE

FLANDERS BROWN ALE, ALSO KNOWN AS OUD BRUIN, IS ONE OF THE WORLD'S GREAT STYLES—COMPLEX, FRUITY, RICH, TART, AND MALTY IN CHARACTER. Historically a "provision," or stock, ale (meaning one meant for laying down, or longer storage) in East Flanders, Oud Bruins are made of blended aged and younger beers (similar to Flemish red), and can be almost sherrylike, with aromas and flavors of raisins, plums, figs, dates, black cherries, caramel, and chocolate. But compared to Flemish reds, Oud Bruins tend to be a bit less acetic, and maltier. With their tart-sweet tastes and malty backbone, they're a blast to sip with the right dish.

Enter *carbonade*. The traditional sour beef and Belgian ale stew, carbonade is one of the most comforting dishes on the planet (sorry, herbivores), and it is still found on seemingly every restaurant menu in *Le Pays de Bière* (that is, Belgium—how cool a nickname is that?). Instead of the classic recipe, which calls for finishing the rich stewed beef with cider vinegar and sugar to get a sweet-sour flavor, we love the effect that a sour brown ale imparts. We found that you need no seasoning other than salt, pepper, and butter when a beer of high quality, like New Belgium's La Folie, is used for the braise.

When we set out to pair the iconic flavors of beef stew and beer in more portable, party-friendly form, we came upon the idea of encasing the stew in a buttery, flaky pastry crust, to create petite pies. Result: You can eat a heavenly stew with one hand and wash it down with a world-class beer in the other. It doesn't get much better.

Makes 16 hand pies

2 LB/910 G BEEF CHUCK ROAST, CUT INTO ½-IN/12-MM CUBES

FINE SEA SALT AND FRESHLY GROUND PEPPER

4 TBSP/55 G UNSALTED BUTTER

2 LARGE YELLOW ONIONS, DICED

2 TBSP ALL-PURPOSE FLOUR

2½ CUPS/600 ML OUD BRUIN BEER

BOUQUET GARNI: 3 FRESH PARSLEY SPRIGS, 3 FRESH THYME SPRIGS, AND 1 BAY LEAF TIED TOGETHER WITH KITCHEN TWINE

DARK BROWN SUGAR AS NEEDED (OPTIONAL)

2 RECIPES PASTRY DOUGH (SEE PAGE 118), CHILLED

1 LARGE EGG BEATEN WITH 1 TSP WATER, FOR AN EGG WASH

1. Pat the beef dry with paper towels and season generously with salt and pepper. Heat a large Dutch oven or other heavy-bottomed pot with a tight-fitting lid over medium-high heat. Add 2 Tbsp of the butter. When the butter is melted and lightly browned, add about one-third of the meat and cook until deeply browned on all sides, 5 to 7 minutes. Avoid stirring for the first 2 to 3 minutes until a nice crust forms on the first side, then stir occasionally. Transfer the browned beef to a bowl. Repeat to brown the rest of the meat in two more batches.

CONTINUED

2. Add the remaining 2 Tbsp butter to the pot, turn the heat to medium, and add the onions. Sauté the onions until browned, 12 to 14 minutes, scraping the browned bits from the bottom and sides of the pot. Stir in the flour until evenly distributed and cook for about 1 minute. Slowly pour in the beer, again scraping the bottom and edges of the pot. Return the beef to the pot, along with any juices accumulated in the bowl. Add the bouquet garni, a big pinch of salt, and pepper to taste. Bring to a simmer, then turn the heat as low as it will go, cover, and cook until the beef is falling-apart tender, stirring and scraping the bottom of the pot occasionally, about 2 hours.

3. Taste and adjust the seasoning. The stew should have a rich, sweet-sour flavor. If you find that it needs a touch more sweetness, add brown sugar, a little at a time, to taste. Pick out and discard the bouquet garni. Let the carbonade cool to room temperature, then refrigerate until chilled, about 2 hours. (The carbonade can be made up to 3 days in advance.)

4. When you are ready to make the hand pies, position racks in the upper and lower thirds of the oven and preheat to 400°F/200°C. Line two large baking sheets with parchment paper.

5. On a lightly floured work surface, roll out one of the discs of pastry dough into a 12-by-16-in/ 30.5-by-40.5-cm rectangle. Trim the shaggy edges and create a neat rectangle using a pastry wheel or pizza cutter. (Save the trimmings to patch up any corners that aren't squared off.) Cut the dough in half lengthwise, then crosswise three times to yield eight 4-by-6-in/10-by-15-cm rectangles. Place a heaping 2 Tbsp of the cold carbonade over half of each rectangle, keeping the other half empty and a ½-in/12-mm border around the edges. Brush the edges lightly with the egg wash and fold the empty half over the filling. Gently pull the edges to make them even, and lightly pinch the seams together. Transfer the pies to one of the prepared baking sheets, spacing them out evenly. Repeat to make another eight pies with the remaining dough disc and carbonade.

6. Press the edges of each pie with the tines of a fork to make a decorative seal, and cut a small *X* on top of each with a sharp paring knife for a steam vent. Brush the tops of the pies lightly with the egg wash. Bake until golden brown and crisp, 25 to 30 minutes, rotating the baking sheets in the oven halfway through. Transfer to wire racks and let cool for at least 5 minutes before serving. Serve hot or at room temperature. (Leftover pies will keep, covered in the refrigerator, for up to 3 days, or wrap them tightly in aluminum foil or freezer wrap and freeze for up to 1 month.)

OUR RECOMMENDED BREWS:

La Folie NEW BELGIUM BREWING / **Petrus Oud Bruin** BAVIK / **The Meddler** ODELL / **Special Reserve** DE DOLLE BROUWERS / **Rosso e Marrone** CAPTAIN LAWRENCE / **Flemish Sour** MONK'S CAFÉ / **Grand Dame** TROIS DAMES

FLEMISH APPLE-BACON TART

BELGIAN STRONG DARK ALE

BELGIAN STRONG DARK BEERS, WHICH HAVE BECOME MORE WIDELY AVAILABLE IN RECENT YEARS—BOTH AS IMPORTS AND CRAFT-BREWED VERSIONS OUTSIDE OF BELGIUM—ARE COMPLEX, FILLING BEERS RICH WITH MALTY SWEET FLAVORS OF RAISIN, PLUM, AND CHERRY, OCCASIONAL SPICINESS, AND A BOOZY KICK. In other words, they are deliciously well suited to many dishes with big flavors. When barrel-aged (although they seldom are), they take on even more complexity and depth. Across Belgium, they are very much at home in the culture of eating and drinking.

It's only fitting to pair a robust Belgian-style ale with Flemish food. And across Flanders, and especially in the French-speaking south, it's part of daily life to gather in *estaminets*, homey cafés with more than the usual culinary options, yet none of the trappings of more formal restaurants. That's the sort of place you'd find this rustic, sweet, and lightly smoky tart, which is as good, if not better, served at a picnic as it is warm from the oven.

Serves 6 to 8

6 OZ/170 G BACON, DICED
1 RECIPE PASTRY DOUGH (SEE PAGE 118), CHILLED
3 LARGE TART APPLES
⅓ CUP/65 G FIRMLY PACKED DARK BROWN SUGAR

1. Preheat the oven to 400°F/200°C. Line a large baking sheet with parchment paper.

2. Heat a sauté pan over medium-high heat. Add the bacon and sauté until crisp and browned but still a little fatty and chewy, 5 to 7 minutes. Transfer the bacon to a plate to cool, using a slotted spoon, reserving the fat in the pan.

3. Roll out the chilled dough on a lightly floured work surface into a 14-by-12-in/35.5-by-30.5-cm rectangle. Roll it up loosely onto the rolling pin and unroll it onto the prepared baking sheet. Tuck about ¾ in/2 cm of the edge of the dough under on all four sides to create an even border; this also creates a double-thick border on the crust. Refrigerate the dough while you prepare the apples.

4. Peel the apples and cut them in half through the stem. Remove the stems and cores with a paring knife and a melon baller. Cut the apples into slices ⅛ in/3 mm thick.

5. Strew the bacon over the dough. Place overlapping slices of apples down the middle of the tart, then continue making rows on both sides of the first row until the dough is covered with apple slices. (Discard the apple ends, which will be awkward to arrange nicely.) Sprinkle the apples evenly with the brown sugar and drizzle with about 2 Tbsp of the bacon pan drippings.

6. Bake until the crust is crisp and golden brown and the edges of the apples start to brown, 35 to 40 minutes, rotating the baking sheet in the oven about halfway through. Transfer to a wire rack to cool. As the tart cools, loosen it with a large spatula once or twice so that any caramelized juices won't stick to the paper. Cut the tart into squares and serve warm or at room temperature.

OUR RECOMMENDED BREWS:

Pannepot DE STRUISE / **Trappistes 8** ROCHEFORT / **Winterkoninkske** BROUWERIJ KERKOM / **Brune** ABBAYE DES ROCS / **Monk's Mistress** MIDNIGHT SUN

GREEN TOMATO AND GOAT CHEESE GALETTE

SAISON

OF ALL THE GREAT BEER STYLES OF THE WORLD, NONE IS MORE FOOD-FRIENDLY THAN SAISON (SEE PAGE 95). The seasonal farmhands in southern Belgium for whom the style is named needed something refreshing to drink during summer and harvest labors, so the brewers of the region made the most of the cool winter and spring months, sometimes adding fresh-picked herbs and greens (like dandelion) and using a voracious, high-temperature yeast that produced grassy, spicy aromas of fresh-cut hay—to this day, sensational with many foods.

Saison is typically 6 to 7% ABV, hazy gold, and highly carbonated, with flavors running a mouth-watering gamut from apricot to lemon to white pepper to banana to clove, and, in the most traditional examples, an overall vinous, fruity tang. Make this rustic French-inspired tart when it's tomato "shoulder season": either in the early summer before the fruits are red and juicy, or when those last few green tomatoes cling to the vine as the weather turns crisp.

This novel preparation of green tomatoes with goat cheese has a good bit of bite balanced by savory herbs and a flaky pastry crust. Look for a classic European saison like Saison d'Erpe-Mere from Brasserie de Glazen Toren, in which nice, long, herbal flavors contrast and complement the tart's (ahem) tartness. In a way, the beer lends another herbal character to the dish.

There are many excellent American saisons, notably from the Commons Brewery, in Portland, Oregon. Their flagship is called Urban Farmhouse, for which they use de Glazen Toren's yeast.

Serves 6

PASTRY DOUGH
¾ CUP/165 G COLD UNSALTED BUTTER, CUT INTO SMALL CUBES
1½ CUPS/180 G ALL-PURPOSE FLOUR
½ TSP FINE SEA SALT
4 TO 6 TBSP/60 TO 80 ML ICE WATER

1½ LB/680 G FIRM, UNDER-RIPE GREEN TOMATOES, CORED AND CUT INTO SLICES ABOUT ¼ IN/6 MM THICK
FINE SEA SALT
1½ TBSP EXTRA-VIRGIN OLIVE OIL
1 GARLIC CLOVE, MINCED
4 OZ/115 G RICOTTA CHEESE
4 OZ/115 G FRESH GOAT CHEESE (CHÈVRE)
1 TSP CHOPPED FRESH SUMMER SAVORY OR THYME
FRESHLY GROUND PEPPER
1 EGG YOLK BEATEN WITH 1 TSP WATER, FOR AN EGG WASH

1. TO MAKE THE DOUGH: Combine the butter, flour, and salt in a food processor and pulse a few times, until the butter chunks are about the size of peas. Add 4 Tbsp/60 ml of the ice water and process very briefly, just to bring the dough together. If it still seems a little dry, add the remaining water 1 Tbsp at a time, pulsing in between additions, just until the dough comes together.

2. Turn the dough out onto a lightly floured work surface and, using the heel of your hand, smear the clumps of dough across the work surface (this technique is called *fraisage* and makes for an incredibly flaky dough). Gather the smeared dough into a mound using a pastry scraper and pat it into a disc. Wrap tightly in plastic wrap and refrigerate for at least 30 minutes, or up to 2 days. (To freeze, wrap it in another layer of plastic wrap and freeze for up to 3 months.)

3. Preheat the oven to 400°F/200°C.

4. Line a baking sheet with paper towels and arrange the tomato slices in a single layer on top. Sprinkle both sides generously with salt and set aside for about 20 minutes to draw out some of the moisture. Blot the tomatoes dry with more paper towels.

5. While the tomatoes are draining, whisk together the olive oil and garlic in a small bowl. Mix together the ricotta, goat cheese, and summer savory in a medium bowl. Season with salt and pepper. Stir about half of the garlic oil into the ricotta mixture.

6. Roll out the chilled dough into a 15-in/38-cm circle using a floured rolling pin. The dough will be quite moist, so rotate it occasionally to be sure it isn't sticking to the work surface, and dust with additional flour as needed. Roll the dough up loosely onto the rolling pin and unroll it onto a large rimmed baking sheet lined with a sheet of parchment paper.

7. Spread the ricotta mixture over the bottom of the dough in an even layer, leaving a 2-in/5-cm border. Layer the tomatoes over the ricotta mixture in concentric circles, starting at the outside and working your way to the center. Drizzle the remaining garlic oil over the tomatoes. Fold in the edges to partially cover the tomatoes, overlapping as needed to create an evenly pleated crust. Brush the crust lightly with the egg wash.

8. Bake the galette until the ricotta is puffy, the tomatoes are slightly wilted, and the crust is golden brown, 35 to 40 minutes. Let cool for at least 15 minutes, or until the galette is at room temperature, then slide onto a cutting board, cut into wedges, and serve.

OUR RECOMMENDED BREWS:

Saison d'Erpe-Mere DE GLAZEN TOREN **/ Urban Farmhouse** THE COMMONS BREWERY **/**
Saison du Fermier SIDE PROJECT **/ Handfarm** TIRED HANDS BREWING COMPANY **/ Hennepin** OMMEGANG

Chapter 5

MALTY, RICH & SWEET

Brewers' malt, which is most commonly made from barley but also is made with some wheats and other grains such as rye, is the backbone of beer. It grows in those famous amber waves, and, when mature, is harvested and "malted"—meaning it's sprouted and carefully dried (see page 13). When that malted grain is boiled in the brewer's kettle, enzymatic transformations occur that make starches fermentable by yeasts, producing carbon dioxide and alcohol. There are hundreds of varieties of such grains; brewers tend to use one or two go-to "base malts," usually pale, to provide the sugars for fermentation. Other brewing grains include oats, wheat, rice, sorghum, and corn, all of which have unique properties of their own · and impart varying flavors and textures to the finished beer.

How deeply these grains are roasted determines the color of the final brew (but note, not strength, which is a factor of the *quantity* of the malt), and much of the beer's flavor components (with other contributions coming from the use of hops, yeast strains, and other additions). What may come as something of a surprise in this chapter is that the recipes we developed for these sweeter, richer beers aren't desserts—save for some seriously delicious Porter Pecan Tassies (page 141).

Instead, what we assembled here are classic international recipes in which the full and sweet flavors of various baked goods, melted sharp cheeses, nuts, caramelized vegetables, crispy fried seafood, and meats glazed with deep fruit flavors meet their ultimate matches in the form of richer beers, from Belgian dubbel, tripel, and quadrupel to English and American barleywines and malty German Märzen, the traditional brew of Munich's Oktoberfest. Offset by deftly administered hops, the buzzy burn of higher alcohol, and brewers' sugars (in the Belgians, especially), the fulsome flavors in these beers aren't about contrasts but complements, matching big flavors pound for pound. Think rich, savory-sweet dishes like French Onion Dip (page 124), Caramelized Cauliflowerets with Hazelnut Romesco Sauce (page 126), and Baby Back Ribs with Burnt Orange Glaze (page 130).

CHIMAY À LA BIÈRE FONDUE

ABBEY ALE

BROADLY SPEAKING, ABBEY ALES ARE MADE UNDER THE WATCH OF MONASTERIES, BUT THESE DAYS IT CAN BE HARD TO DISCERN WHAT BEER COMES FROM A TRUE TRAPPIST ABBEY, BREWED UNDER DIRECT SUPERVISION OF, AND SOMETIMES BY, THE MONKS (LOOK FOR THE WORDS "AUTHENTIC TRAPPIST PRODUCT"), AND WHAT IS MERELY PRODUCED IN ASSOCIATION WITH A GIVEN ABBEY (FAR MORE COMMON). And then there are beers with no connection to real holy places whatsoever. What you need to know is that abbey beers tend to be malt-forward, spicy-tasting beers, generally called *dubbel*, *tripel*, or *quadrupel*, which are references to old brewing measurements of grain (and thus correspond still to strength).

Fondue is, of course, one of the most enjoyable party dishes imaginable. It can make an ordinary evening unforgettable. Traditionally made with white wine and Gruyère or other Swiss alpine cheeses, this version is made with an abbey-style beer *and* an abbey-style cheese, Chimay à la Bière, with a beer-washed rind. Instead of the usual winey flavors, beer fondue abounds in ripe yet earthy, mellow hop bitterness and the kick of a stronger Belgian-style ale. Watch the beer-blessed celebrants dive in.

Serves 6 to 8

ONE 12-OZ/360-ML BOTTLE BELGIAN ABBEY ALE SUCH AS CHIMAY RED OR OMMEGANG ABBEY

1 LB/455 G CHIMAY À LA BIÈRE OR OTHER WASHED-RIND CHEESE SUCH AS TALEGGIO OR ROBIOLA, RINDS TRIMMED AND DISCARDED, FINELY CHOPPED

2 TBSP CORNSTARCH

2 TSP DIJON MUSTARD

DASH OF WORCESTERSHIRE SAUCE

PINCH OF PAPRIKA

FINE SEA SALT

SOFT PRETZELS (SEE PAGE 138), GRILLED SAUSAGES, SLICED TART APPLES, AND/OR PICKLED VEGETABLES FOR SERVING

1. Bring the ale to a boil over medium heat in a fondue pot or a heavy-bottomed 2-qt/2-L saucepan. Turn the heat to medium-low.

2. Combine the cheese and cornstarch in a medium bowl and toss to coat. Add the cheese to the ale a large handful at a time, stirring in a figure-eight pattern until the cheese is completely melted before each addition. Have patience; this could take a total of 20 minutes and it is important that the cheese melts slowly and completely.

3. When all of the cheese is melted and the fondue is thick, stir in the mustard, Worcestershire sauce, and paprika. Season with salt.

4. Serve piping hot, from the fondue pot placed over a low flame or the saucepan set on a trivet. (If you're serving it from a saucepan, you'll need to return it to a low flame to remelt the cheese once it begins to solidify. Do this stirring gently, again in a figure-eight pattern.) Offer your guests forks or metal skewers for dipping the pretzels, sausages, apples, or vegetables.

OUR RECOMMENDED BREWS:

Grande Réserve ("Blue") CHIMAY / Achel 8 Blond ACHEL / Bush du Nuits (Scaldis Prestige) DUBUISSON / Interlude ALLAGASH / Grand Cru ABBAYE DES ROCS

FRENCH ONION DIP

WHETHER YOU'VE GOT FRIENDS GATHERED FOR A BALL-GAME ON TV OR AROUND THE CARD TABLE, OR ARE HOSTING A COMPLETELY SOPHISTICATED SALON, THIS RETRO PARTY DIP IS ALWAYS A WINNER, ESPECIALLY WHEN IT'S MADE FROM SCRATCH WITH REAL CARAMELIZED ONIONS. Of course, you could serve it with a bag of crinkle-cut potato chips, but spears of fresh, crisp vegetables are a refreshingly lighter way to go.

The best beer for this throwback revival is going to bring some assertive malts to the party, as in English, Scottish, and American brown and red ales. In a great nut brown, there's a mellow, slightly sweet, caramelly nuttiness that works perfectly with caramelized onions. If you live in Wisconsin, you're probably a fan of Fat Squirrel, available, alas, only in-state. AleSmith of San Diego makes a delicious nut brown that's exceptionally smooth and clean finishing, cutting through the fattiness a bit, while a hoppier brown ale, such as Schooner Exact's King Street Brown, is more assertive.

Serves 6 to 8

4 TBSP/55 G UNSALTED BUTTER

2 TBSP PEANUT OIL OR VEGETABLE OIL

2 LARGE SWEET YELLOW ONIONS, CUT INTO ¼-IN/6-MM DICE

1 TSP FINE SEA SALT

⅛ TSP CAYENNE PEPPER

4 FRESH THYME SPRIGS

1 CUP/240 ML SOUR CREAM

4 OZ/115 G CREAM CHEESE, AT ROOM TEMPERATURE

2 TSP ONION POWDER

FRESH CRUDITÉS SUCH AS CARROTS, CELERY, RADISHES, AND BELGIAN ENDIVE FOR SERVING

1. Melt the butter in the peanut oil in a 12-in/30.5-cm sauté pan over medium-high heat. Add the onions, salt, and cayenne and sauté until the onions are translucent, the liquid they release has evaporated, and they begin to fry, about 10 minutes. Turn the heat to medium-low and cook, stirring occasionally, until the onions are evenly browned and meltingly soft, 25 to 30 minutes longer. Tuck the thyme sprigs into the caramelized onions, remove the pan from the heat, and set aside to let cool completely.

2. Combine the sour cream, cream cheese, and onion powder in the bowl of an electric mixer fitted with the paddle attachment and beat until smooth. Pick out and discard the thyme sprigs from the onions, add the onions to the bowl, and beat to mix well. Taste and adjust the seasoning.

3. Serve at room temperature, with the crudités for dipping. (Leftover dip will keep, tightly covered in the refrigerator, for up to 5 days.)

OUR RECOMMENDED BREWS:

Nut Brown ALESMITH / King Street Brown SCHOONER EXACT / Nut Brown FULL SAIL / Angry Boy Brown BAIRD BREWING CO. / 12 Days HOOK NORTON

STILTON WELSH RAREBIT
WITH FIG JAM

OLD ALE

NO, THIS IS NOT RABBIT, IT'S RAREBIT, A PLAY ON THE FORMER BUT NONETHELESS MEATLESS. Our wee version of the immensely satisfying eighteenth-century English-tavern fare of melted cheese on toast is magnificent as either an appetizer or an encore bow to an evening of beer tasting. While many a malty British beer would work well, we heartily endorse a barleywine or old ale of 9 to 12% ABV to match the Stilton's ultra-ripe acidity and the fig jam's sweetness.

"Old ale," formerly known as "stock ale," is typically a deep amber brew with fruity, vinous notes of raisin and black currants, almost port- or sherrylike in character. For an authentic British version, look for Ola Dubh Special Reserve from Harviestoun (any you can find). Two of the best American specimens we've come across are North Coast's Old Stock Ale (11.8% ABV) and Upright Brewing Company's Billy the Mountain (9.1% ABV), both from the West Coast. The most traditional versions play up the old barrel notes, to recapture the flavor that old ales were still famous for in the early eighteenth century. Almost any old or stock ale can be aged for a time, if you've got the patience.

Serves 6 to 8

¼ CUP/60 ML SOUR CREAM
2 EGG YOLKS
2 TBSP OLD ALE
1 TSP DRY YELLOW MUSTARD POWDER
¼ TSP FRESHLY GROUND PEPPER
DASH OF WORCESTERSHIRE SAUCE
6 OZ/170 G STILTON CHEESE, CRUMBLED
1 BAGUETTE
ABOUT ⅓ CUP/110 G FIG JAM

1. Position the broiler rack about 6 in/15 cm from the heat source and preheat the broiler.

2. Whisk together the sour cream, egg yolks, ale, mustard, pepper, and Worcestershire sauce in a small bowl. Add the cheese and mash and stir with a fork until the mixture forms a creamy, slightly chunky sauce.

3. Cut the baguette crosswise on the diagonal into 16 to 18 slices about ½ in/12 mm thick. (You may not use the whole loaf.) Arrange the slices on a large baking sheet, place it under the broiler, and toast the baguette slices until the edges are golden brown, 1 to 2 minutes.

4. Spread the toasted side of the baguette slices with a thin layer of fig jam, then top with a thick coating of the cheese mixture, dividing it evenly and spreading it all the way to the edges to completely cover the bread. Place them back on the baking sheet and return to the broiler just until the cheese is evenly blistered and melted, 1 to 1½ minutes. Let cool for a few minutes, then serve warm.

OUR RECOMMENDED BREWS:

Old Stock Ale NORTH COAST BREWING CO. / **Billy the Mountain** UPRIGHT BREWING / **Bois** THE BRUERY / **Adam** HAIR OF THE DOG / **Ola Dubh Special Reserve** HARVIESTOUN

CARAMELIZED CAULIFLOWERETS
WITH HAZELNUT ROMESCO SAUCE

TRIPEL

WE ASSURE YOU THAT *CAULIFLOWERETS* IS A REAL WORD, REFERRING TO THE TINY TREE SHAPES YOU GET WHEN A HEAD OF CAULIFLOWER IS BROKEN APART. We also assure you that Belgian tripel, a flaxen-hued ale of anywhere from 8 to 12% ABV, with abundant fruity aromas, is named for an old Trappist brewing measurement indicating three times the single, or *simple*, serving of grain. It's fortified with up to 25 percent Belgian brewing sugar, which lightens body while amping up alcohol and complexity, and is often sold in 750-ml bottles with a wire cork-and-cage enclosure. Due to its sweetness, tripel isn't exactly a popular beer style to pair with foods, but it can be terrific.

In this robust Spanish sauce, with its complex combination of acidic, sweet, nutty, and salty flavors, the full-flavored tripel meets its match. The caramelized starches in seared cauliflower echo sweet malts in the beer, while the alcohol and slight tangy snap achieve a perfect parity in the romesco.

Serves 4 to 6

ROMESCO SAUCE

1 DRIED ANCHO (SOMETIMES CALLED PASILLA) CHILE

1 LARGE RIPE TOMATO, DICED, OR ⅓ CUP/85 G CANNED DICED TOMATOES

2 TBSP SHERRY VINEGAR, PLUS MORE AS NEEDED

¼ CUP/40 G ROASTED HAZELNUTS

2 GARLIC CLOVES

1 ROASTED RED BELL PEPPER (JARRED OR HOMEMADE), STEMMED AND SEEDED

2 TBSP DRIED BREAD CRUMBS

1 EGG YOLK

KOSHER OR SEA SALT

3 TBSP EXTRA-VIRGIN OLIVE OIL

1 LARGE HEAD CAULIFLOWER, TRIMMED AND CUT INTO 2-IN/5-CM FLOWERETS

4 TBSP/60 ML EXTRA-VIRGIN OLIVE OIL, PLUS MORE AS NEEDED

FINE SEA SALT

1 TBSP CHOPPED FRESH PARSLEY

1. TO MAKE THE ROMESCO SAUCE: Slit the dried chile lengthwise and discard the stem and seeds. Chop it into little pieces and place in a small bowl with the tomato and vinegar. Let stand until softened, about 30 minutes.

2. Combine the hazelnuts and garlic in a food processor and pulse until finely minced. Add the tomato mixture, roasted pepper, bread crumbs, egg yolk, and 1½ tsp salt and process the mixture to a coarse purée, scraping down the sides of the bowl as needed. With the machine running, slowly drizzle in the olive oil through the feed tube and process until smooth and emulsified. Stop the machine and taste; add more salt or vinegar as needed. (The romesco will keep in the refrigerator, tightly covered, for up to 3 days.)

3. Bring a large pot of generously salted water to a boil over high heat. Add the cauliflower and cook for 2 minutes. Immediately drain the cauliflower, then transfer to a kitchen towel and pat dry.

4. Heat two large skillets over medium-high heat (or cook the cauliflower in two batches). Add 2 Tbsp of the olive oil to each pan. When you just begin to see wisps of smoke, add the cauliflower and a big pinch of salt. Spread the cauliflower in a single layer in the pan and cook, without disturbing, until deeply browned on the first side, 3 or 4 minutes. Turn and cook until the second side is deeply browned, 3 or 4 minutes longer. If the pans become dry, add more oil as needed.

5. Transfer the seared cauliflower to a platter and garnish with the parsley. Serve hot or at room temperature, with the romesco sauce in a small bowl on the platter for dipping.

OUR RECOMMENDED BREWS:

Tripel Karmeliet BROUWERIJ BOSTEELS **/ Long Strange Tripel** BOULEVARD **/ Guldenberg** DE RANKE **/ Tripel Van De Garre** BROUWERIJ VAN STEENBERGE **/ Watou Tripel** BROUWERIJ ST. BERNARDUS

CHICKPEA FRIES
WITH PIMENTÓN MAYO

BIÈRE DE GARDE

THESE FRIES ARE SO DELECTABLE, YOU'LL HAVE TO RESTRAIN YOURSELF FROM EATING A FULL PLATE. Served hot, they scream for a beer pairing that not only accentuates the smoky flavor and subtle heat of the mayo, but refreshes the palate with every sip.

An ideal beer to pair with this dish is the amber-hued bière de garde (see page 108), characterized by malty softness and delicate spicy character. Like its geographical and stylistic neighbor saison, it's a complex draught; but whereas true saisons show off flowery, spicy aromas, in bière de garde the malt comes to the fore, a perfect match for the mild sweetness in these rich chickpea fries. It's a versatile, refreshing, not-too-filling brew with a nice, lacy head of foam that is harmonious with the smoky pimentón mayo, too.

Serves 4 to 6

1½ CUPS/180 G CHICKPEA FLOUR
FINE SEA SALT
1 TBSP OLIVE OIL, PLUS MORE FOR FRYING
¼ CUP/7 G FINELY CHOPPED FRESH PARSLEY
1 CUP/240 ML MAYONNAISE
½ TSP SMOKED SPANISH PAPRIKA (PIMENTÓN)
1 LEMON, CUT INTO WEDGES

1. Line a small rimmed baking sheet with parchment or wax paper.

2. Bring 2 cups/480 ml water to a boil in a medium saucepan over medium-high heat. Remove from the heat and slowly pour in 1 cup/120 g of the chickpea flour, whisking constantly to prevent lumps from forming. Stir in 1 tsp salt and return the mixture to the stove top. Turn the heat to medium and cook, stirring constantly, until the batter has a very thick and gloppy consistency and pulls away from the sides and bottom of the pan, about 1 minute. Remove the pan from the heat and stir in the olive oil and about half of the parsley. Taste and adjust the seasoning.

3. Pour the chickpea mixture onto the prepared baking sheet. Spread into an even, square-shaped layer about ⅜ in/1 cm thick, using a spatula and dipping it in hot water as needed to prevent sticking. Cover with parchment paper or plastic wrap and refrigerate to cool and set, at least 30 minutes or up to 24 hours.

4. Meanwhile, stir together the mayonnaise and paprika in a small bowl. Cover and refrigerate. (The sauce will keep, covered in the refrigerator, for up to 1 week.)

5. When you are ready to make the fries, pour olive oil into a large skillet to a depth of about ½ in/12 mm and heat over medium heat. The oil is ready for frying when a small crumb of the chickpea batter sizzles enthusiastically when it's dropped in. Place a platter lined with paper towels near the stove top.

6. Cut the chickpea cake into long, thin strips, like hand-cut french fries. Put the remaining ½ cup/60 g chickpea flour in a large bowl and gently toss the fries in it to coat evenly.

7. Working in batches to avoid crowding, carefully place the fries in the hot oil. Fry, turning occasionally with a slotted metal spatula, until crisp on the outside, 3 to 5 minutes. Transfer the fries to the prepared platter and immediately sprinkle with salt. Squeeze the juice from the lemon wedges over the fries, sprinkle with the reserved parsley, and serve hot with the pimentón mayo for dipping.

OUR RECOMMENDED BREWS:

Avant Garde Ale LOST ABBEY / Cuvée des Jonquilles AU BARON / Blonde Bière de Garde CASTELAIN / Ambrée LA CHOULETTE / La Bavaisienne Blonde THEILLIER

DRUNKEN CHICKEN HEARTS

BELGIAN DUBBEL OR STRONG DARK/ABBEY ALE

RICH AND FULSOME, THIS BUCOLIC ENGLISH DISH WILL SUCCEED WHERE FEAR DOES NOT, BY TAKING AN OFT-OVERLOOKED ORGAN MEAT AND RENDERING IT NOT ONLY PERFECTLY UNINTIMIDATING, BUT DELICIOUS.

Chicken hearts are returning to fashion at restaurants that pay particular attention to "variety meats," and more and more often they can be found in a well-stocked butcher's case next to chicken livers, legs, and thighs at many higher-end supermarkets. Or, just ask for them.

With concentrated chicken flavor, chewy texture, and less of the taste of iron you find in chicken livers, the hearts have deep flavors that commingle in a rare way with the cherry jam and cayenne pepper. Paired with a solidly alcoholic abbey ale, the stewed chicken hearts, which appealingly resemble a pile of sautéed mushrooms on croutons of crusty bread, are wintry, warming, and buzzy to boot.

Serves 4

2 TBSP DUCK FAT OR UNSALTED BUTTER
1 LB/455 G CHICKEN HEARTS, RINSED, PATTED DRY, AND HALVED LENGTHWISE
FINE SEA SALT
½ CUP/120 ML ABBEY ALE
3 TBSP CHERRY JAM
1 TBSP CIDER VINEGAR
1 TBSP DIJON MUSTARD
¼ TSP FRESHLY GROUND BLACK PEPPER
PINCH OF CAYENNE PEPPER
DASH OF WORCESTERSHIRE SAUCE

2 TBSP SOUR CREAM
3 TBSP COARSELY CHOPPED FRESH PARSLEY
4 SLICES WHITE BREAD, TOASTED

1. Heat a 12-in/30.5-cm sauté pan over medium-high heat, then add the duck fat. When the fat is melted and sizzling hot, add the chicken hearts, season them generously with salt, and sauté until browned and firm but still pink inside, about 4 minutes. Transfer the hearts to a bowl using a slotted spoon, reserving the fat in the pan.

2. Add the ale, jam, vinegar, mustard, black pepper, cayenne, and Worcestershire sauce to the pan and bring the mixture to a boil over medium-high heat. Cook, stirring occasionally, until the sauce is reduced by three-fourths, about 5 minutes. Stir the hearts back in, along with any juices accumulated in the bowl, and continue cooking until the sauce is thickened and coats the hearts nicely, 2 to 4 minutes longer.

3. Stir in the sour cream and cook for 1 minute. Remove from the heat and stir in the parsley. Arrange the toasted bread on a platter or individual plates, spoon the hearts and sauce over, and serve immediately.

OUR RECOMMENDED BREWS:

Brother Thelonius Abbey Dubbel NORTH COAST BREWING CO. / Strong Dark PFRIEM / Generaal VICARIS / Dubbel WESTMALLE / Barrel Aged Ovila Dubbel SIERRA NEVADA / Grand Cru GREEN FLASH

BABY BACK RIBS
WITH BURNT ORANGE GLAZE

QUADRUPEL OR BARLEYWINE

AFTER STEAM-ROASTING UNTIL TENDER IN A SPICED ORANGE-MARMALADE MARINADE, MORE MARMALADE IS BRUSHED ON THESE SUCCULENT RIBS AND CARAMELIZED UNDER THE BROILER, TO CREATE A GLAZE THAT'S AT ONCE SWEET AND A TAD BITTER FROM THE ORANGE PEELS.

The total effect hugely complements barleywines and quadrupels that, soaring over 10% ABV, burst with deep, treacly sugars, spicy yeasts, boozy burn, and bitterness in awe-inspiring balance. Belgian-style "quads" tend to have more peppery yeasts, while viscous barleywines, which emerged in England, range from merely fruity to marmalade-like in their own right.

Serves 4 to 6

2 RACKS BABY BACK RIBS, ABOUT 5 LB/2.3 KG TOTAL WEIGHT
1 CUP/300 G ORANGE MARMALADE
¼ CUP/60 ML QUADRUPEL OR BARLEYWINE
¼ CUP/60 ML SOY SAUCE
2 TBSP WORCESTERSHIRE SAUCE
4 LARGE GARLIC CLOVES, GRATED OR PRESSED
1 TBSP PEELED AND GRATED FRESH GINGER
1 TBSP FINE SEA SALT
1 TSP FRESHLY GROUND PEPPER
¼ TSP GROUND CINNAMON
¼ TSP FRESHLY GRATED NUTMEG
⅛ TSP GROUND CLOVES

1. Arrange the rib racks with the meaty sides down in a large glass or ceramic baking dish. Whisk together ¼ cup/75 g of the marmalade, the beer, soy sauce, Worcestershire sauce, garlic, ginger, salt, pepper, cinnamon, nutmeg, and cloves in a medium bowl. Pour the marinade over the ribs and spread it around to coat, allowing most of it to pool in the bottom of the dish. Cover with aluminum foil and let marinate in the refrigerator for at least 4 hours, or preferably overnight.

2. Preheat the oven to 300°F/150°C. Place the ribs, still in the baking dish covered with foil, in the oven and steam-roast until the meat gives easily when pierced with a fork, but is not quite falling off the bone, about 2½ hours. Remove the ribs from the oven.

3. Switch the oven to the broil setting and position an oven rack on the lowest rung. Transfer the ribs from the baking dish to a large rimmed baking sheet lined with aluminum foil, meaty-side down, and set aside while the broiler preheats.

4. Meanwhile, whisk together the remaining ¾ cup/ 225 g marmalade and ⅓ cup/75 ml of the hot pan drippings in a small bowl; discard the remaining pan drippings. Brush the tops of the ribs, or bone side, with a generous coating of the glaze. Place the baking sheet in the oven on the lowest rack and broil until the glaze is caramelized and the edges of the ribs begin to blacken, 5 to 7 minutes. Flip the ribs over so that the meaty side is now up and brush with a thick coating of the glaze. Return the ribs to the bottom rack and broil until caramelized and just beginning to blacken, about 5 minutes. Carefully brush with a second coating of glaze, and continue broiling until deeply caramelized and blackened in spots, about 5 minutes longer.

5. Transfer the rib racks to a cutting board, tent loosely with foil, and rest for about 10 minutes. Carve the racks into individual ribs. Pile on a large platter and serve immediately, with plenty of napkins.

OUR RECOMMENDED BREWS:

The Stoic DESCHUTES BREWERY / Trappistes 10 ROCHEFORT / ImmortAle DOGFISH HEAD / Mother of All Storms PELICAN / The Sixth Glass BOULEVARD

CHINATOWN SHRIMP TOASTS
WITH SWEET-AND-SOUR ALE SAUCE

`TRIPEL`

EASY LIKE A SUNDAY MORNING . . . SHRIMP TOASTS HAIL FROM THE AMERICANIZED DIM SUM BRUNCH TRADITION OF SUPER-STEAMING-HOT, FLAVOR-PACKED SMALL PLATES YOU WANT AFTER A BIG SATURDAY NIGHT, WHEN YOUR BODY'S CRAVING SALT, SUGAR, AND, LET'S FACE IT—MORE BEER. Our clever twist on this retro Chinatown snack makes use of sour ales in the ubiquitous sweet-and-sour sauce, which is traditionally made with pineapple juice. So use assertively tart and sour tropical or exotic fruit sour ales, if you can spare them. As for what to drink as you throw back one after another of these fried flavor bombs, we found success with a nice tripel. The rich, sugary body complemented the sweet and sour sauce and fried bread, while tangy, hoppy, and herbal notes found a friend in the oceanic shrimp spread.

Serves 6 to 8

SWEET-AND-SOUR ALE SAUCE

1 TBSP CORNSTARCH

1 TBSP TART, FRUITY WILD AMERICAN ALE OR FLANDERS RED ALE, PLUS ⅔ CUP/165 ML

½ CUP/100 G FIRMLY PACKED LIGHT BROWN SUGAR

⅓ CUP/75 ML RICE VINEGAR

2 TBSP KETCHUP

1 TBSP SRIRACHA SAUCE

1 TBSP SOY SAUCE

5 SLICES STALE WHITE OR WHEAT SANDWICH BREAD, CRUSTS TRIMMED TO PERFECT SQUARES

3 GREEN ONIONS, WHITE AND LIGHT GREEN PARTS ONLY; 1 COARSELY CHOPPED AND 2 THINLY SLICED ON THE DIAGONAL

2 GARLIC CLOVES

ONE ½-IN/12-MM PIECE GINGER, PEELED

8 OZ/225 G SHRIMP, PEELED AND DEVEINED

½ CUP/75 G WATER CHESTNUTS

½ CUP/15 G LIGHTLY PACKED FRESH CILANTRO LEAVES

1 TBSP SOY SAUCE

1 TSP SESAME OIL

½ TSP FINE SEA SALT

¼ TSP FRESHLY GROUND PEPPER

1 EGG WHITE, LIGHTLY BEATEN UNTIL FOAMY

BLACK SESAME SEEDS FOR SPRINKLING

PEANUT OIL OR VEGETABLE OIL FOR FRYING

1. TO MAKE THE SAUCE: Dissolve the cornstarch in 1 Tbsp ale in a small bowl; set aside. Stir together the ⅔ cup/165 ml ale, brown sugar, vinegar, ketchup, Sriracha, and soy sauce in a small saucepan and bring to a full boil over medium-high heat. Whisk in the cornstarch slurry and cook until the sauce thickens nicely, about 2 minutes. Remove from the heat and let the sauce cool to room temperature. Taste and adjust the seasoning. (The sauce will keep, tightly covered in the refrigerator, for up to 2 weeks.)

2. If the bread isn't sufficiently stale, place it on a wire rack set on a rimmed baking sheet and bake at 200°F/95°C until mostly dried but still just a little soft in the center.

3. Put the chopped green onion, garlic, and ginger in a food processor and pulse until finely minced. Scrape down the sides of the bowl as needed. Add the shrimp, water chestnuts, cilantro, soy sauce, sesame oil, salt, and pepper and pulse until the mixture is a very coarse paste with chunks of shrimp and water chestnut still visible (not finely puréed). Stir in the beaten egg white.

4. Spread the mixture thickly on each slice of bread, dividing it evenly. Sprinkle with the sesame seeds. Freeze the shrimp toasts until slightly firm, about 20 minutes, then quarter them diagonally to make 20 triangles.

5. Pour peanut oil into a 12-in/30.5-cm skillet to a depth of ½ in/12 mm and heat over medium-high heat. Line a large baking sheet with paper towels and set it near the stove. When the oil reaches 325°F/165°C, or when a crumb of bread sizzles enthusiastically, gently add half of the toasts, shrimp-side down. Fry, turning once, until golden on both sides and the shrimp is cooked through and crusty, about 2 minutes per side. Adjust the heat as needed to maintain the oil temperature. Transfer the toasts to the paper towels and repeat to fry the rest.

6. Arrange the toasts on a large platter and garnish with the sliced green onions. Serve immediately, with the sweet-and-sour sauce in a small bowl on the side for dipping.

OUR RECOMMENDED BREWS:

Golden Monkey VICTORY / **New World Tripel** BOSTON BEER COMPANY / **La Fin du Monde** UNIBROUE / **Tripel** BROUWERIJ WEST / **Bink Tripel** KERKOM

BUTTERMILK FRIED OYSTERS
WITH HORSERADISH RÉMOULADE

BELGIAN STRONG ALE & TRIPEL

BELGIAN STRONG ALES, AS THE NAME SUGGESTS, ARE BIG BEERS (8 TO 9% ABV) WITH THE SPICY KICK OF BELGIAN YEAST. The most famous of all is a classic, Duvel, brewed since 1871 and known in the 1920s as Victory, but dubbed "duvel" (dialect for "devil") for its sneaky strength. With its massive effervescence and assertive bitterness, it's a bracing beer with much to offer, though there are relatively few foods that can match its power.

The late beer writer Michael Jackson said it best, "Duvel defies categorization. It is a beer in a style of its own creation. It has none of the heaviness of a barleywine, for example, or the crude flavors of a head-banging lager. If this Devil were a pugilist, it would be a boxer rather than a fighter. In the absence of an agreed category, its many imitators in Belgium are reduced to indicating their intentions by having brand-names that suggest devilment, roguishness or scallywaggery."

Fried oysters, an occasion unto themselves, certainly can match this brew punch for punch. This opulent New Orleans classic is extra special served in Belgian endive spears for a handy delivery mechanism, which in turn echoes the faint, spicy background bitterness in the beer. Meanwhile, the oyster proteins take on deep, mineral, umami-like flavors when cooked, which the beer's tang seems to enhance, adding to the interplay of the flavorful dip and crispy, salty breading.

Serves 4 to 6

RÉMOULADE

½ CUP/120 ML MAYONNAISE

2 TBSP MINCED CORNICHONS OR DILL PICKLES

1 TBSP PREPARED HORSERADISH

1 TBSP CAPERS, DRAINED, RINSED, AND MINCED

1 TBSP MINCED FRESH PARSLEY

1 TBSP MINCED SHALLOTS

1 TSP SHERRY VINEGAR

½ TSP PAPRIKA

FINE SEA SALT AND FRESHLY GROUND PEPPER

1 CUP/140 G FINE CORNMEAL OR CORNFLOUR

½ CUP/60 G ALL-PURPOSE FLOUR

1½ TSP OLD BAY SEASONING

FINE SEA SALT

1 CUP/240 ML BUTTERMILK

16 SMALL OYSTERS, SHUCKED

PEANUT OIL OR VEGETABLE OIL FOR FRYING

3 LARGE BELGIAN ENDIVES, TRIMMED AND SEPARATED INTO LEAVES

CONTINUED

1. TO MAKE THE RÉMOULADE: Stir together the mayonnaise, cornichons, horseradish, capers, parsley, shallots, vinegar, and paprika in a small bowl. Season with salt and pepper. Set aside while you fry the oysters. (The rémoulade will keep, covered tightly in the refrigerator, for up to 3 days.)

2. Whisk together the cornmeal, flour, Old Bay seasoning, and 1 tsp salt in a shallow bowl. Pour the buttermilk into another shallow bowl. Dip the oysters one at a time in the buttermilk, and then dredge them in the cornmeal mixture, patting gently to help it adhere and coat evenly. Collect the breaded oysters on a wire rack as you work.

3. Pour peanut oil into a large skillet to a depth of ¾ in/2 cm and heat over medium-high heat. When the oil reaches 350°F/180°C, or when a crumb of breading sizzles enthusiastically, gently add some of the oysters, being careful not to over-crowd the pan. Fry, turning once, until golden and crisp on both sides, about 2 minutes per side. Transfer the fried oysters to paper towels to drain and sprinkle with salt while still warm. Repeat to fry the remaining oysters, adjusting the heat as needed to maintain the oil temperature and allowing it to return to 350°F/180°C between batches.

4. Arrange the 16 largest endive leaves on a serving platter (reserve the small inner leaves for another use). Spoon a dollop of the rémoulade into the wide, cuplike end of each leaf. Nestle a fried oyster on the sauce and serve immediately.

OUR RECOMMENDED BREWS:

Duvel DUVEL MOORTGAT **/ Tripel Reserve** ALLAGASH **/ The Tide & Its Takers** ANCHORAGE BREWING CO. **/
Xtra Gold** CAPTAIN LAWRENCE **/ Super Baladin** LE BALADIN

IRISH OATCAKES

OATMEAL STOUT

"MAY YOUR HOME ALWAYS BE TOO SMALL TO HOLD YOUR FRIENDS," GOES THE CLASSIC IRISH TOAST. What a pleasant idea, right? That is, provided one has plenty of rations. Enter the easy but iconic Irish oatcake, which works deliciously as an icebreaker, but is perhaps best as the delivery system for a wedge of cheese at the end of a casual evening. With their chewy texture and unassuming appearance, they're rather simple—but highly satisfying washed down with a nice beer, especially served right out of the oven with a good, aged Irish Cheddar and a dollop of marmalade.

Oatcakes are reassuring, substantial, and wonderfully old-fashioned—anything but ostentatious. On the best nights, a timely round with the right friends might even beckon a bit of what Yeats called "the Celtic Twilight": pleasurable melancholy expressed through storytelling, searching for truths that can't be expressed. Anyone who has had a beer in one of the great, traditional pubs of Ireland will relate.

In this dish, white Cheddar invites pairing with many styles of beer, from porter to dry stout or even a wee heavy barleywine. But it's the roasty but not too potent oatmeal stout, with a silkiness derived from additions of oats in the brewing process, that makes for a delicious and sociably light matchup.

Makes 12 individual cakes

1⅓ CUPS/115 G ROLLED OATS, PLUS MORE FOR DUSTING
1 CUP/120 G WHOLE-WHEAT FLOUR
1 TSP FINE SEA SALT
1 TSP GRANULATED SUGAR
¼ TSP BAKING POWDER
¼ CUP/55 G LARD OR BUTTER, CUT INTO SMALL PIECES
½ CUP/120 ML COLD WATER
1 TBSP MILK
1 TSP POWDERED SUGAR
TWELVE 2-IN/5-CM SQUARE SLICES AGED IRISH WHITE CHEDDAR
ORANGE MARMALADE FOR SERVING

1. Position a rack in the center of the oven and preheat to 325°F/165°C. Lightly butter a large baking sheet.

2. Place the rolled oats, flour, salt, granulated sugar, and baking powder in a food processor and pulse briefly to combine. Add the lard and process until evenly distributed in fine pieces. Transfer the mixture to a large bowl and drizzle in the cold water. Use a fork to mix the dough just until it's evenly moistened. Gather the dough into a ball and pat it into a thick disk.

3. Sprinkle rolled oats lightly over a large wooden cutting board or a clean work surface. Using a rolling pin, roll out the dough to a ¼-in/6-mm thickness. Cut out circles with a 3-in/7.5-cm round cookie cutter and place them on the prepared baking sheet. Mix together the milk and powdered sugar in a small bowl until the sugar dissolves. Brush the top of each oatcake lightly with the milk mixture. Bake until the oatcakes are dry on top and crisp on the bottom, about 25 minutes.

4. Transfer the oatcakes to a wire rack to cool slightly, then arrange them on a platter and top each with a Cheddar slice. Serve immediately, with a small dish of marmalade on the side for spooning on top.

OUR RECOMMENDED BREWS:

Velvet Merlin FIRESTONE WALKER / **Oatmeal Stout** SCHLAFLY; SAMUEL SMITH; BELL'S / **Oatis** NINKASI

BAVARIAN SOFT PRETZELS

OKTOBERFEST MÄRZEN

TO A BEER LOVER, THERE'S NOTHING BETTER THAN FALL. First come the seasonal samplings, often of bigger beers in cozy beer halls with friends. Then there are the serious parties, like Munich's Oktoberfest, which since the early nineteenth century have commemorated events as historical as a beer-soaked royal wedding party. For Germans, Oktoberfest is a national institution; 70 percent of attendees are local, and consumption tops 15 million pints. The traditional Bavarian seasonal brew is Märzen ("mahr-tsen"), a full-flavored, deep gold–to–amber lager with an assertive but smooth, toasty malt character and the taste (but not aroma) of delicately spicy hops. Historically brewed in March and aged in ice caves over the summer, Märzen has been the victim of a perplexing indifference in Munich—it's not even readily served at the Oktoberfest, where lighter beers seem the only choice. Fortunately, though, you can still find them in the best beer halls, bottle shops, and many grocery stores around the United States. They're smooth, elegant, and warming, with an alcohol content of 5 to 7% ABV, ideal for washing down this perfect pretzel.

Andrea traversed the globe to research the recipe that follows—from the *biergartens* of Bavaria to the historic bakeries of Pennsylvania Dutch Country, where pretzels first landed in America from the Old World in the late nineteenth century. (The recipe first appeared in her book *Pretzel Making at Home*.)

Get ready for real German soft pretzels: the iconic knot; the leathery, deep mahogany crusts showered with crunchy salt; and that *je ne sais quoi* flavor that can only be described as "pretzely." It's that texture, color, and flavor that sets pretzels apart from other yeasted breads, and it's traditionally derived from a rather peculiar source: lye. But in this home-cook-friendly version, we spare you the hazardous chemical cookery and offer up a suitable alternative: baked baking soda. When baking soda is placed in a low oven, the heat alters its chemistry, making it more similar to lye and giving your pretzels that oh-so-authentic appeal.

Makes 8 pretzels

PRETZEL DOUGH

2¼ TSP ACTIVE DRY YEAST

½ CUP/120 ML WARM WATER (BETWEEN 100° AND 115°F/38° AND 45°C)

1 TBSP BARLEY MALT SYRUP OR DARK BROWN SUGAR

3¼ CUPS/390 G UNBLEACHED BREAD FLOUR, PLUS MORE AS NEEDED

½ CUP/120 ML COLD MÄRZEN

2 TBSP UNSALTED BUTTER, CUT INTO SMALL CUBES, AT ROOM TEMPERATURE

2 TSP FINE SEA SALT

¼ CUP/70 G BAKING SODA

1 EGG YOLK BEATEN WITH 1 TBSP WATER, FOR AN EGG WASH

COARSE SEA SALT FOR SPRINKLING

1. TO MAKE THE DOUGH: Sprinkle the yeast over the warm water in a large bowl or the bowl of a stand mixer. Stir in the barley malt syrup until dissolved. Let the mixture stand until the yeast blooms and is a little foamy, 5 to 7 minutes. Add the flour, beer, butter, and fine salt to the yeast mixture and stir to form a shaggy mass. Begin kneading with the dough hook on medium-low speed or on a lightly floured countertop with your hands. After about 1 minute, the dough will form a smooth ball. It should be quite firm and may be slightly tacky but not sticky. If it is sticky, add a little more flour, about 1 Tbsp at a time, and knead

CONTINUED

in until the dough is smooth. If the dough is too dry to come together, add more water, 1 tsp at a time. Continue kneading the dough on medium-low speed or by hand until smooth and elastic, 5 to 7 minutes. Transfer the dough to a large, lightly greased bowl, cover with plastic wrap, and refrigerate for at least 8 hours, or up to 24 hours, for optimal flavor.

2. Meanwhile, preheat the oven to 250°F/120°C. Spread the baking soda in a small baking dish and bake for about 1 hour. Remove from the oven and let cool. Store the baking soda in an airtight container until ready to use.

3. When you are ready to shape the pretzels, line two large baking sheets with aluminum foil and coat them well with nonstick cooking spray.

4. Turn the dough out onto an unfloured work surface and firmly press it down to deflate. To form the classic pretzel shape, cut the dough into eight equal portions. Working with one piece of dough at a time and keeping the rest covered, pat the dough down into a rough rectangle, then tightly roll it up length-wise, forming it into a little loaf. Pinch the seam. Shape the dough into a rope by rolling it against the work surface, applying mild pressure and working from the center of the dough out. If you need more friction, spray the counter with a little water from a squirt bottle or drizzle with a few drops of water and spread it with your hand. Once you can feel that the dough rope doesn't want to stretch any farther (usually when it is between 12 to 16 in/ 30.5 to 40.5 cm long) set it aside to rest and begin shaping another piece in the same manner. Repeat this process with the remaining pieces of dough.

5. Return to the first dough rope and continue rolling it out to a length of 24 to 28 in/60 to 70 cm, leaving the center about 1 in/2.5 cm in diameter and thinly tapering the ends by applying a little more pressure as you work your way out. Position the dough rope into a "U" shape with the ends pointing away from you. Holding one of the ends in each hand, cross the dough and then cross it again. Fold the ends down and press them into the *U* at

about four and eight o'clock, letting about ¼ in/ 6 mm of the ends overhang. Place the pretzel on one of the prepared baking sheets and cover with a damp kitchen towel. Repeat this process with the remaining dough pieces, spacing the pretzels out on the baking sheets at least 1 in/2.5 cm apart.

6. Let the pretzels rise at warm room temperature until increased in size by about half, 20 to 30 minutes. (The pretzels can be covered tightly with plastic wrap and refrigerated for up to 8 hours at this point.)

7. Position racks in the upper and lower thirds of the oven and preheat to 500°F/260°C.

8. Select a large, stainless-steel pot that is at least 2 in/5 cm wider than the diameter of the pretzels and tall enough so that the water will come up no more than 3 in/7.5 cm from the rim. (Avoid non-stick and other metal surfaces, such as aluminum and copper, which may react with the baking soda.) Turn the hood vent on high and put on a pair of rubber dishwashing gloves, and avoid splashing the soda water you are about to make on your skin or in your eyes.

9. Put the baked baking soda in the pot and pour in 6 cups/1.4 L water. Bring the water to a low simmer over high heat, stirring gently to dissolve. Lower the heat to maintain a very gentle simmer. Using a large skimmer, gently dip the pretzels in the simmering liquid, one or two at a time. Leave them in the solution for about 20 seconds, carefully turning once after about 10 seconds. Lift and strain them from the liquid using a skimmer, allowing the excess to drip off, and return the pretzels to the baking sheets, again spacing them at least 1 in/2.5 cm apart as you work. If the ends detach, simply reposition them. Repeat with the remaining pretzels.

10. Quickly brush the tops of the pretzels lightly with the egg wash and sprinkle with coarse salt.

11. Bake the pretzels immediately until deep mahogany in color, 9 to 12 minutes, rotating the baking sheets from front to back and top to bottom half-way through the baking time. Transfer the pretzels to a wire rack to cool for about 10 minutes before serving.

OUR RECOMMENDED BREWS:

Oktober Fest-Märzen AYINGER / SurlyFest SURLY / Hoss Rye Lager GREAT DIVIDE / Octoberfest FREE STATE / Oktoberfest Märzen PAULANER

PORTER PECAN TASSIES

ENGLISH PORTER

PORTER, A FULL-BODIED, CHOCOLATEY BROWN ALE, BECAME POPULAR WITH MEMBERS OF THE TRANSPORTATION INDUSTRY IN LONDON DURING THE 1700S, AND WAS SERVED IN A FEW VARIATIONS OF STRENGTH AND HUE, BASED ON COMBINATIONS OF NEW, OLD, AND MILD ALES BLENDED TOGETHER. The modern version we think of is marked by rich flavors of cocoa and caramel, although typically it's neither extremely sweet nor bone dry.

"Tassie" is either old Scottish for "little cup," or Middle French, from the French word *tassette*, a small pocket, pouch, or cup. Or something else, perhaps; no one seems too sure. But how we think of it now is as a diminutive, wintry tart cup made with nuts (typically pecans) and a crumbly, buttery crust that has an irresistible texture and lingering sweetness. Like pecan pie poppers, they make felicitous dessert bites around the holidays, especially spiked with a splash of English porter.

Makes 16 tassies

DOUGH

½ CUP/110 G UNSALTED BUTTER, AT ROOM TEMPERATURE

3 OZ/85 G CREAM CHEESE, AT ROOM TEMPERATURE

1 CUP/120 G ALL-PURPOSE FLOUR

PINCH OF FINE SEA SALT

FILLING

½ CUP/100 G FIRMLY PACKED DARK BROWN SUGAR

¼ CUP/60 ML PORTER

1 TBSP ALL-PURPOSE FLOUR

1 LARGE EGG

1 TSP PURE VANILLA EXTRACT

¼ TSP FINE SEA SALT

¾ CUP/75 G PECANS, CHOPPED, PLUS 16 WHOLE PECANS

2 TBSP UNSALTED BUTTER, MELTED

1. TO MAKE THE DOUGH: Combine the butter, cream cheese, flour, and salt in a stand mixer fitted with the paddle attachment and beat on low speed until well blended. Divide the dough into 16 pieces and press each piece into the bottom and up the sides of a cup in a mini muffin pan. Cover with plastic wrap and refrigerate until firm, about 30 minutes.

2. Preheat the oven to 350°F/180°C.

3. TO MAKE THE FILLING: Whisk together the brown sugar, porter, flour, egg, vanilla, and salt in a large bowl. Add the chopped pecans and melted butter and stir to mix well. Evenly divide between the dough cups, then top each with a whole pecan.

4. Bake until the crust edges are golden brown and the filling is set, 40 to 50 minutes. Let cool for about 10 minutes in the muffin cups. While the tassies are still warm, run a knife around the edges and invert the pan onto a cooling rack to release them from the pan. (They will stick to the pan if left to cool completely.) Turn them right-side up on a wire rack and let cool completely before serving. (The tassies can be stored in an airtight container in the refrigerator for up to 4 days.)

OUR RECOMMENDED BREWS:

London Porter YOUNG'S / London Porter MEANTIME / Publican Porter SHORT'S / Cutthroat Porter ODELL / London Porter PROPELLER / Two Penny Porter BAD ATTITUDE

Chapter 6

DEEP, ROASTY & SMOKY

And now we come to the end—of the beer flavor spectrum, that is. The delicious beers in this chapter, like rich Bordeaux blends, French roast coffee, and long-aged spirits, top the scale of big flavor. Colors range, generally, from umber to onyx (with one surprisingly smoky blond to keep things interesting). These are likely to be among the most demanding, substantial, and memorable beers you'll encounter, and the recipes we chose to go with them, which range from delicate homemade potato chips to several stunning desserts, will help you discover just how interesting ultra-rich, dark craft beer can be with the *right* foods.

As we described in the introduction to chapter 5, beer's color is determined by the degree to which the malt is kilned, and how much of it the brewer uses in proportion to other grains. Take barley malt and roast it just until lightly colored, and you'll be brewing some sort of pale ale. Roast it to a milk-chocolate brown and the flavors, rather miraculously, taste of cacao to match. Go deeper into midnight hues and the flavors that emerge range from a straight shot of espresso to a side of soy sauce (and we mean that in a good way). What this does not determine is strength. As we noted in chapter 1, Guinness is actually a light beer; and likewise, the black lagers in this chapter are actually light bodied, if deep in flavor.

Aging beers in barrels that once contained wine, whiskey, or other spirits has become a potent symbol and a measure of innovation in craft breweries around the world. Executed without care, the boozy flavors in the wood can easily overwhelm whatever beer had the misfortune to be siphoned in, and a promising brew will emerge months (or years) later as a beery clone of the former tenant. Done well, however, as with the beers in this chapter, and the best of those barrels comes forth: grace notes of tobacco, vanilla, spice, oak, and a vinous acidity that can balance the biggest, most syrupy strong stouts.

Some specialty brewers' malt may be smoked over peat or alderwood branches, and the flavors in beers made with those range from last night's campfire to creosote on a train trestle warmed in the hot summer sun. From roasty black lagers to dark roasted maple porters, stouts, and imperial stouts to smoked beers and doppelbocks, this is the land of big, distinctive beers with hugely assertive flavors.

Foodwise, the smokiness of dishes like Grilled Eggplant Rolls with Cucumber Labneh (page 150) and those iconic Bamberg Onions (page 148) are an obvious match to smoky beers. Roasty, toasty brews marry well with sweet, full flavors, in both savory-sweet preparations like Split Pea Fritters with Grade B Maple Syrup (page 145) and dessert sweets like a festively whimsical Chocolate Salami (page 160). The latter, we assure you, makes a grand finale to a delicious, beer-filled evening . . . and to this book.

BBQ BAKED SWEET POTATO CHIPS

PORTER

THE SECRET TO EXECUTING THIS (RELATIVELY) HEALTHFUL PARTY PLEASER IS USING A GOOD, SHARP MANDOLINE, A TABLETOP CONTRAPTION USED TO CUT VEGETABLES INTO IMPOSSIBLY, DELICATELY THIN SLICES. They are available in a range of prices, and are an invaluable tool for any cook—for example, they can also be used to make french fries (see page 85)!

This recipe is a gift. Whereas store-bought BBQ chips are greasy, loaded with suspect colorings and chemicals, these baked slices of sweet potato have an appealing substantiality and crunch, along with a zingy blend of BBQ spices.

These fiery, lingering spicy flavors require a bigger beer, so look no further than porter, the chocolatey, roasty-tasting dark ale London made famous in the eighteenth century. So-called American porter retains the style's historically supple body and flavors of dried cocoa, coffee, and caramel, but adds lashings of fruity esters; citrusy, floral hops; and a dry, refreshing finish. Deschutes' Black Butte Porter is a breakout for the brewery that continues to be among the best-selling porters in the United States.

Serves 4 to 6

1½ LB/680 G ORANGE-FLESHED SWEET POTATOES, SUCH AS JEWEL OR GARNET, PEELED

2 TBSP EXTRA-VIRGIN OLIVE OIL

1¼ TSP FINE SEA SALT

1 TSP CHILI POWDER

½ TSP SWEET PAPRIKA

¾ TSP DARK BROWN SUGAR

¼ TSP FRESHLY GROUND BLACK PEPPER

⅛ TSP GROUND CUMIN

⅛ TSP GARLIC POWDER

⅛ TSP ONION POWDER

PINCH OF CAYENNE PEPPER

1. Position racks in the upper and lower thirds of the oven and preheat to 275°F/135°C.

2. Slice the sweet potato 1/16 in/2 mm thick, or as thinly as possible, using a mandoline. The important thing is to get an even thickness.

3. Put the potatoes in a large bowl, drizzle with the olive oil, sprinkle with 1 tsp of the salt, and toss gently to coat evenly, making sure that none of the potato slices are sticking together; you want every slice coated on both sides.

4. Arrange the potato slices in a single layer on two large rimmed baking sheets; the edges can overlap a little because the slices will shrink in the oven. Bake until dry and just beginning to brown, flipping the slices once about halfway through. (The chips won't become crisp and crunchy until after they cool.) The time it takes depends on the thickness of the potatoes, but it should be 1 to 1½ hours; start checking after 45 minutes and remove any chips that are done before the rest.

5. Meanwhile, sift the chili powder, paprika, brown sugar, black pepper, cumin, garlic powder, onion powder, cayenne, and remaining ¼ tsp salt into a bowl.

6. Immediately transfer the hot chips to a large bowl and sprinkle with the seasoning mix. Toss gently to coat evenly. Let cool completely. Store in an airtight container at room temperature for up to 1 week.

OUR RECOMMENDED BREWS:

Black Butte Porter DESCHUTES BREWERY / **Payback Porter** SPEAKEASY / **Porter** NØGNE Ø / **CoCoNut PorTer** MAUI BREWING CO. / **Barrel Aged People's Porter** FOOTHILLS

SPLIT PEA FRITTERS
WITH GRADE B MAPLE SYRUP

WEE HEAVY; SCOTCH ALE

SCOTLAND'S UNFORGIVING ELEMENTS, AMONG OTHER FACTORS, LED TO A FONDNESS FOR STRONG DRINK. And whoever said strong beer can't make for a great breakfast was wrong. In this sweet and savory pairing for hearty souls, the sweetness of Scotch ale, also known as wee heavy, melds seamlessly with fragrantly stewed split peas. This is as it should be, especially in that season as winter yields to warmer months.

Adding an unexpected splash of deep, sweet flavor to fried delights is like going from two people to three on a trampoline—a lot of fun. An English barleywine will pair nicely; but in the case of this dish, one beer in particular is remarkably well matched. Dieu du Ciel!, a brewery in Montreal, can seem to do no wrong, with a wide mastery of styles across the flavor spectrum. Their Équinoxe du Printemps Scotch Ale (8% ABV) has the heft and brogue of the best wee heavies, but adds grace notes of Québécois maple syrup harvested in spring.

Serves 4

1 TBSP OLIVE OIL

2 LARGE SHALLOTS, FINELY CHOPPED

1 MEDIUM CARROT, PEELED AND FINELY CHOPPED

1 CELERY STALK, FINELY CHOPPED

2 GARLIC CLOVES, MINCED

1½ CUPS/360 ML GOOD-QUALITY LOW-SODIUM CHICKEN STOCK OR VEGETABLE STOCK

½ CUP/100 G YELLOW SPLIT PEAS

4 FRESH THYME SPRIGS

1 BAY LEAF

1 TSP FINE SEA SALT

¼ TSP FRESHLY GROUND PEPPER

½ CUP/60 G ALL-PURPOSE FLOUR

1 LARGE EGG, BEATEN

½ CUP/55 G FINE DRIED BREAD CRUMBS

PEANUT OIL OR VEGETABLE OIL FOR FRYING

GRADE B MAPLE SYRUP FOR DRIZZLING

1. Heat the olive oil in a small saucepan over medium heat. Add the shallots, carrot, celery, and garlic and sauté until soft, about 6 minutes. Add the chicken stock, split peas, thyme, and bay leaf and bring to a boil over high heat. Lower the heat to maintain a low simmer, cover partially, and cook until the split peas are tender and beginning to break down, 35 to 40 minutes. (If the liquid is absorbed before the split peas are cooked, add a little water, about ¼ cup/60 ml at a time.) Stir in the salt and pepper and continue cooking, stirring often and adjusting the heat as needed, until the split peas are a thick and chunky mush, 10 to 15 minutes longer.

2. Line a rimmed baking sheet with parchment or wax paper. Pour the split pea mixture onto the parchment paper, spread it in an even layer, and set aside until completely cooled, at least 30 minutes.

CONTINUED

3. Put the flour in a shallow bowl, the egg in a second shallow bowl, and the bread crumbs in a third shallow bowl; line the bowls up in that order. With slightly wet hands, form the cooled split pea mixture into balls, each about 1½ in/4 cm in diameter.

4. One or two at a time, toss the balls in the flour to coat. Dip them in the egg, letting the excess drip off. Finally, toss them in the bread crumbs and gently pat on the breading to help it adhere and coat evenly. Arrange the fritters on a large baking sheet as you work. When all of the fritters are coated, put the baking sheet in the refrigerator for about 20 minutes.

5. Pour peanut oil into a large pot to a depth of ¾ in/2 cm and heat over medium-high heat until a deep-fry thermometer registers 375°F/190°C. Line a baking sheet with paper towels and set it near the stove.

6. Lower some of the fritters into the hot oil, being careful not to overcrowd the pot, and fry until golden brown and crunchy on all sides, 3 to 5 minutes, adjusting the heat to maintain the temperature of the oil. Remove the fritters with a slotted spoon and transfer them to the prepared baking sheet to drain. Allow the oil to return to 375°F/190°C, then repeat to fry the remaining fritters. Arrange the fritters in a shallow serving bowl, drizzle with the maple syrup, and serve hot.

OUR RECOMMENDED BREWS:

Équinoxe du Printemps DIEU DU CIEL! **/ Maple Bacon Coffee Porter** FUNKY BUDDHA **/ Maple Pecan Porter** BOSTON BEER COMPANY **/ Scotch Ale** SMUTTYNOSE

BAMBERG ONIONS

RAUCHBIER

ONE OF THE GREAT DRINKING CITIES IN THE WORLD— ALONG WITH PORTLAND, OREGON, AND BRUSSELS, BELGIUM—BAMBERG, GERMANY, IS A CITY DEFINED BY ITS BREWING INDUSTRY. With impossibly picturesque Baroque architecture, the entire town, nestled along the Regnitz river in the Upper Franconia section of Bavaria, is listed as a UNESCO World Heritage site. But it's what you'll find inside the atmospheric, wood-stove-warmed *bierstubes* that makes it truly one of a kind.

Where there's smoke, there's fire. Gathered with friends inside a *bierstube*, with its low ceiling, exposed beams, worn wooden tables, and thick leaded-glass windows, you truly feel the embrace of Germanic beer culture, as hospitable as it comes. And Bamberg's famed export, *rauchbier*, or "smoke beer," is the campfire everyone gathers around. The deep amber beer, made with malts smoked over peaty beechwood, bears the unmistakable, almost overpowering, taste of smoke. Hardly a contemporary touch, this is in fact how many beers once tasted. Before the popularization, in the eighteenth century, of using modern, indirect kilns for drying malt, brewers' grains were smoky, even charred. The flavors disappeared from most breweries, but in Bamberg, two operations persisted, and have loyal followings to this day. Spezial and Schlenkerla are world famous for their smoked beers, as charry and rich as bacon in a glass.

The saying in Bamberg is that you need to drink a few liters or more of these numbers before you fully appreciate the style. We don't think it takes nearly that much. At Schlenkerla, a fine place to discover an appreciation, there's a menu to match their appeal, as old-fashioned as a steam train. One local specialty is the *Bamberger Zwiebel in Rauchbiersoße mit Kartoffeln,* a massive onion stuffed with spiced pork, served with mashed potatoes and a pan sauce made with the rauchbier.

The sheer size of that famous comfort-food dish, at least as they prepare it, is a bit daunting, so we pared it down to small-plate size. In the United States, look for onions that are about 2 in/5 cm in diameter—Vidalia onions are a good choice. We also recommend using Schlenkerla's weizen or helles in the recipe rather than the more famous Märzen, which, while delicious, turns aggressively bitter when cooked. As for what to drink with a serving or two, by all means, Schlenkerla's helles and Märzen are both excellent, as are stronger beers such as the now-classic Alaskan Smoked Porter, made since 1988 in Juneau, with malts hand-smoked over alderwood branches.

Serves 8

8 SMALL WHITE, YELLOW, OR VIDALIA ONIONS, ABOUT 2 LB/910 G TOTAL WEIGHT (SEE RECIPE INTRODUCTION)

6 SLICES THICK-CUT SMOKED BACON, DICED

2 LARGE EGGS

8 OZ/230 G GROUND PORK

1 CUP/60 G FRESH BREAD CRUMBS

¼ CUP/7 G CHOPPED FRESH PARSLEY

2 TSP CHOPPED FRESH MARJORAM OR OREGANO

FINE SEA SALT

1 TSP FRESHLY GROUND PEPPER

⅛ TSP FRESHLY GRATED NUTMEG

1 CUP/240 ML GOOD-QUALITY LOW-SODIUM BEEF STOCK

1½ TBSP WONDRA INSTANT FLOUR

1 CUP/240 ML SCHLENKERLA RAUCHBIER (SCHLENKERLA SMOKED BEER)

1. Preheat the oven to 375°F/190°C.

2. Trim about ½ in/12 mm off the top of each onion to prepare it for hollowing out into a bowl shape. Reserve the tops for later. Cut about ½ in/12 mm off the root ends (so they will stand up in the baking dish) and peel the onions. Hollow out the onions by cutting and scooping out (using a paring knife and spoon) the center layers until you are left with a shell about ¼ in/6 mm thick. (After digging out some of the onion, you should be able to stick your finger through the root end and push the center layers out the top.) Set the hollowed onions upright in a Dutch oven or skillet just large enough to fit them all snugly.

3. Finely dice enough of the onion innards to make about 1 cup/150 g. Heat a sauté pan over medium heat. Add the bacon and diced onions and sauté until lightly browned, 7 to 8 minutes. Set aside to cool for a few minutes.

4. Beat the eggs in a large bowl, then add the ground pork, bread crumbs, parsley, marjoram, 1 tsp salt, pepper, nutmeg, and cooked bacon-onion mixture. Using your hands, mash everything together to make the stuffing.

5. Spoon the stuffing into the onion shells, packing it in and mounding it on top to use it all up. Pour the beef stock into the bottom of the Dutch oven, cover, and roast until the onions are mostly tender and the stuffing appears cooked but pale on top, about 30 minutes. Uncover and continue roasting until the stuffing is lightly browned and the onions are very tender, about 30 minutes longer. Transfer the onions to a platter using a slotted spoon and cover with aluminum foil. Turn off the oven and place the platter inside to keep the onions hot while you make the sauce.

6. Whisk the flour with 1½ Tbsp water in a small bowl to make a smooth paste. Slowly whisk in a splash of the beer to thin it and make sure the flour is fully dissolved.

7. Place the Dutch oven with the stock over medium-high heat and bring to a boil. Whisk in the flour mixture, then the remaining beer and bring to a simmer. Lower the heat to maintain a bare simmer and cook until the flavors meld and the sauce has thickened enough to coat the back of a spoon, about 5 minutes. Season the sauce with salt.

8. Pour the sauce around the onions, not on top of them, so that it pools on the bottom of the platter. Serve immediately.

GRILLED EGGPLANT ROLLS
WITH CUCUMBER LABNEH

SMOKED HELLES LAGER

LABNEH—A POPULAR FOOD OF THE LEVANT, OR EASTERN MEDITERRANEAN COUNTRIES, PARTICULARLY ISRAEL— IS MADE BY STRAINING THE WHEY FROM YOGURT TO GET A THICKENED VERSION THAT IS ESSENTIALLY FRESH, HOMEMADE CHEESE. Here, we mix this vibrant cheese with cool cucumber and mint, briny olives, and garlic to fill smoky grilled eggplant slices. The fresh combination is sure to be a new go-to for outdoor entertaining.

Eggplant on the grill really absorbs and amplifies smoky tastes, so for this dish, we chose the smoked pale lager from Aecht Schlenkerla, a brewery in Bamberg, Germany, famous for its heavier smoked lagers (see more on their rauchbier on page 148). Of all their smoke-tinged brews, their helles is arguably the most delicious. Its faint hint of campfire—derived, the story goes, from being brewed with the same equipment used for the other, bigger, smokier beers, though not from actual smoked malt—works beautifully with the olive and tang of labneh. Hops are not too prevalent here, and the beer's clean, dry finish leaves us wanting more every time. This is not a style that many breweries have made successfully, but Schlenkerla is a revelatory exception.

Serves 4 to 6

1 CUP/240 ML GREEK-STYLE YOGURT

2 LARGE GLOBE EGGPLANTS

FINE SEA SALT

3 TBSP EXTRA-VIRGIN OLIVE OIL, PLUS MORE FOR DRIZZLING

½ MEDIUM CUCUMBER

¼ CUP/40 G FINELY CHOPPED KALAMATA OLIVES

1 SMALL GARLIC CLOVE, MINCED

1 TBSP JULIENNED FRESH MINT

½ TSP ALEPPO OR OTHER SWEET, MILD CHILE POWDER, PLUS MORE FOR GARNISH

1. Line a fine-mesh sieve with two layers of cheese-cloth and set it over a bowl. Add the yogurt, cover loosely with the overhanging cheesecloth, and refrigerate until thickened, at least 8 hours or up to 24 hours. You should end up with a heaping ½ cup/160 g of labneh. (If you want to make more labneh to have on hand for other uses, just start with more yogurt.)

2. Trim the ends of the eggplants and cut them lengthwise into slices ¼ in/6 cm thick. Arrange the slices in a single layer on a large baking sheet lined with paper towels. Season both sides generously with salt, and set aside for about 30 minutes to draw out some of the moisture. Blot the eggplant dry, then brush on both sides with the olive oil.

CONTINUED

3. Prepare a hot fire in a charcoal grill or preheat a gas grill to high. Arrange the eggplant slices on the grate and grill until tender but not mushy, and deep, charred marks appear, about 2 minutes per side. Set aside to let cool completely.

4. Grate the cucumber on the largest holes of a box grater into a medium bowl. Add the labneh, olives, garlic, mint, ½ tsp salt, and chile powder and stir it all together to make the filling.

5. Spoon a heaping 1 Tbsp of the filling onto the narrow end of each slice of grilled eggplant. Roll the eggplant up into roulades, enclosing the filling snugly. Arrange the roulades, seam-side down, on a platter as you work. Drizzle with olive oil, sprinkle with a little more chile powder, and serve immediately.

OUR RECOMMENDED BREWS:

Helles AECHT SCHLENKERLA **/ Smoke Screen Helles Lager** BALLAST POINT

ROASTED DELICATA SQUASH
WITH ROBIOLA AND BACON BITS

LICHTENHAINER/GRÄTZER

ONCE, MOST BEER WAS SOUR AND SMOKY, OWING TO PRIMITIVE TECHNIQUES OF DRYING MALT IN THE OPEN AIR, BUT THAT DOESN'T MEAN IT WAS UNDRINKABLE. Still, the worldwide shift to clear, gold lagers in the 1840s pushed a lot of lesser-known regional specialties off the shelves. Thankfully those obscure styles have not completely disappeared. What German brewer Sebastian Sauer has done in recent years is lead a mini-movement to rediscover and reinterpret the flavors of some forgotten styles that were made along these lines. His Abraxxxas beer is an example of Lichtenhainer, a sort of German pale ale brewed with smoked malt, lightly soured with *Lactobacillus*.

Two related styles are the all-wheat-based grodziskie, a.k.a. grätzer, and gose, which is a moderately sour, salted, coriander-spiced ale from Leipzig. Many American craft brewers have been playing with the styles, even Samuel Adams (Boston Beer Co.). And what to eat with this specialty? We loved this quick and simple squash dish, which is a bit like stuffed potato skins, only classier. You'll love how the faint sourness and smoky flavors of the beer match its super-funky robiola cheese and smoked bacon goodness.

Serves 6 to 8

3 DELICATA SQUASH, ABOUT 2½ LB/1.2 KG TOTAL WEIGHT
2 TSP EXTRA-VIRGIN OLIVE OIL
½ TSP FINE SEA SALT
½ TSP PIMENT D'ESPELETTE (OPTIONAL)
3 SLICES THICK-CUT BACON, FINELY CHOPPED
6 OZ/170 G ROBIOLA CHEESE, THINLY SLICED

1. Arrange a rack in the upper third of the oven and preheat to 400°F/200°C.

2. Halve the squash lengthwise and scoop out the seeds. Cut each half crosswise into thirds to make 18 squash cups. Pile the squash on a large baking sheet. Drizzle with the olive oil, sprinkle with the salt and piment d'Espelette (if using), and toss to coat evenly. Arrange the squash so it's evenly spaced on the pan, cup-side up. Sprinkle the bacon into the hollow of each squash cup, dividing it evenly. Roast until the squash is tender and the bacon is crisp, 30 to 35 minutes.

3. Remove the baking sheet from the oven and switch the oven to broil. Lay a slice of cheese over the bacon in each squash cup, return to the oven, and broil until the cheese is melted and the edges of the squash are blistered, 2 to 3 minutes. Serve hot or at room temperature.

OUR RECOMMENDED BREWS:

Abraxxxas FREIGEIST BIERKULTUR / **Grätzer** WESTBROOK / **Son of a Batch Dark Gose** THE MONARCHY / **First Sparrow** WHITE BIRCH

HUARACHES
WITH BLACK BEANS, GREEN CHILES, AVOCADO, AND RADISH SLAW

SCHWARZBIER (BLACK LAGER)

IN THIS FUN, SAVORY NUEVO LATINO VARIATION ON TRADITIONAL MEXICAN STREET FARE, A CRISP TWICE-GRIDDLED MASA CAKE SERVES AS THE FOUNDATION FOR A BLOCK PARTY OF FLAVORS. Layered with earthy black beans, crumbly Mexican cheese, a crunchy cabbage and radish slaw, and bright notes of lime and cilantro, it's moderately complex in flavor and execution but completely satisfying, filling, and perfect for a lunch fiesta with friends. Best of all, as you might guess, the appealing rustic shape resembles (more or less) the famous leather sandal for which the dish is named.

To pair, we recommend a clean and light-bodied but roasty schwarzbier, or black lager, a style that originated in Germany's Thuringia and Saxony and dates back to the late 1300s. With earthy roasted malt and occasionally a very slight percentage of smoked malt, schwarzbier is a deceptively light lager-style beer, traditionally just 4 to 5% ABV. The flavors of espresso-like roasted malt work well with the earthy, rich beans, while the beer's faint acidity and hoppiness complement the bright tang of cabbage, cilantro, and lime. If you decide to spice up your huarache to a higher degree, you could slide into India black ale territory, but we found delicious results with a schwarzbier like Mönchshof Schwarzbier, from Kulmbach, Germany, or, for an American craft-brewed version, Heater Allen's, from Oregon.

Serves 6

4 CUPS/360 G LOOSELY PACKED FINELY SHREDDED GREEN CABBAGE

1½ CUPS/175 G INSTANT CORN MASA FLOUR (MASA HARINA)

1½ TSP FINE SEA SALT

½ CUP/120 ML MEXICAN CREMA OR SOUR CREAM

1 CUP/30 G LOOSELY PACKED FRESH CILANTRO, THIN STEMS AND LEAVES

5 GREEN ONIONS, WHITE AND LIGHT GREEN PARTS ONLY; 1 COARSELY CHOPPED AND 4 THINLY SLICED ON THE DIAGONAL

1 SERRANO CHILE, STEMMED AND COARSELY CHOPPED

1 TBSP FRESH LIME JUICE

ONE 15-OZ/425-G CAN BLACK BEANS, DRAINED AND RINSED

½ TSP GROUND CUMIN

1 BUNCH RADISHES, TRIMMED AND VERY THINLY SLICED

ONE 4-OZ/115-G CAN DICED GREEN CHILES

⅔ CUP/70 G FRESHLY GRATED QUESO ANEJO OR OTHER DRY GRATING CHEESE SUCH AS MANCHEGO OR PARMIGIANO-REGGIANO

VEGETABLE OIL FOR FRYING

2 RIPE AVOCADOS, PITTED, PEELED, AND THINLY SLICED

1. Submerge the cabbage in a large bowl of ice water for about 30 minutes to make it extra crunchy.

2. Stir together the masa and ½ tsp of the salt in a medium bowl. Pour in 1 cup plus 1 Tbsp/255 ml hot tap water to make a crumbly dough. Cover the bowl with plastic wrap and set aside.

CONTINUED

3. Combine the crema, cilantro, chopped green onion, serrano chile, lime juice, and ½ tsp salt in a food processor and process to a smooth sauce. Transfer to a small bowl and set aside.

4. Put the black beans in the food processor (no need to rinse it out first) along with the cumin, remaining ½ tsp salt, and ⅓ cup/75 ml water and process until completely smooth. Add another splash of water if needed to loosen the consistency. Transfer the bean spread to a small bowl and set aside.

5. Wet your hands and briefly knead the masa into a smooth, moist dough. Divide the dough into six balls and cover them with plastic wrap. They should be very smooth and cohesive with no cracks; if not, wet your hands again and briefly knead in a little more water. Line a tortilla press with two pieces of plastic wrap, or have ready two pieces of plastic wrap and a rolling pin.

6. You will first shape the huaraches and cook them on a griddle to dry the dough and set the shape, then you will griddle them a second time in oil to brown and crisp them before topping and serving. Heat a large, dry griddle or cast-iron skillet over medium heat. Form one ball of dough into a cylinder about 3 in/7.5 cm long. Place it between the two pieces of plastic wrap and press or roll it out to an oval about ⅛ in/3 mm thick. (If the edges are jagged, the dough is too dry. Knead a little more water into the dough and try again.)

7. Place the huarache on the griddle and cook until dry and slightly crackly on both sides, about 2 minutes per side. Continue shaping the huaraches and griddling as many as you can at a time until they are all cooked. Arrange them on a large baking sheet as you work. When all of the huaraches are cooked for the first time, cover with plastic wrap and set aside. (At this point they can be refrigerated, wrapped tightly, for up to 1 day before finishing and serving.)

8. Preheat the oven to 200°F/95°C.

9. Drain and dry the cabbage in a salad spinner or kitchen towel. Combine the cabbage, radishes, and thinly sliced green onions in a large bowl, and toss to mix. Drizzle in enough of the cilantro sauce to coat lightly and toss in. Set aside.

10. Have ready the bean spread, green chiles, and grated cheese. Heat the griddle over medium-high heat and pour in enough vegetable oil to coat thinly. When you just begin to see wisps of smoke, add as many huaraches as will fit comfortably on the griddle. Cook until crisp and lightly browned on the bottom, 1 to 2 minutes. Flip them over and top with a thick smear of the bean spread, some of the chiles, and a sprinkling of cheese. Cook until the bottom and edges are crisp and lightly browned, about 2 minutes more. Transfer the huaraches to a large rimmed baking sheet and place in the oven to keep warm while you cook the remaining dough.

11. Top each huarache with slices of avocado, then a pile of the slaw, and serve immediately. Pass the remaining sauce at the table for drizzling.

COFFEE STOUT TIRAMISÙ

COFFEE STOUT

INVENTED IN TREVISO AT EL TOULÀ, A HOTEL RESTAU-RANT NOTED FOR ITS GOOD COOKING, THIS SIMPLE DESSERT HAS BECOME SO FAMOUS IN AMERICA THAT IT SEEMS TO APPEAR ON EVERY MENU IN THE LAND. The word *tiramisù* literally means "pick-me-up"—perhaps a reference to its caffeine content. Many recipes add booze—in the form of Marsala, rum, grappa, or a coffee-flavored liqueur—but suppos-edly, the original was nonalcoholic.

We won't be making that one. Instead, look for a strong coffee stout, which brewers make by adding coffee beans or actual brewed or steeped coffee to each batch. The most full-flavored examples are barrel-aged, too, in casks that once contained bourbon, like Goose Island's Bourbon County Coffee Stout. Each year Goose Island teams up with a different specialty coffee roaster, and each year the bottles disappear quickly into the hands of collectors. But many excellent versions can be found in good bottle shops. Look for one with more alcohol, such as in an imperial stout, because those sharper, almost winelike notes offset the rich cocoa and espresso-like flavors from roasted malts and coffee beans. Ideally, the barrel-aged versions taste of vanilla, wood, caramel, and spice, too.

This version of tiramisù comes in individual serving sizes, perfect for a party. Use wide-mouth half-pint glass canning jars, or similarly sized cups, to build imperfectly perfect layers of whipped egg, mascarpone cheese, and stout-soaked pound cake. It's rich, it's potent, and it's a great way to end an evening.

Serves 6

1 VANILLA POUND CAKE
1½ CUPS/360 ML COFFEE STOUT
2 LARGE EGGS, SEPARATED
⅓ CUP/65 G SUGAR
½ CUP/110 G MASCARPONE, AT ROOM TEMPERATURE
COCOA POWDER FOR DUSTING

1. Trim the end crusts from the pound cake, then cut 12 slices, each about ½ in/12 mm thick. Use a round cutter to cut out circles from each slice roughly the diameter of the jars or cups in which you will build the individual tiramisùs.

2. Pack one slice into the bottom of each of six jars and drizzle 2 Tbsp of the stout over each. Set the remaining slices of pound cake aside.

3. Beat the egg whites in the clean, dry bowl of a stand mixer fitted with the whisk attachment, or in a large bowl with a hand-held electric mixer, until stiff peaks form.

4. Whisk the egg yolks in a medium bowl until well blended. Add the sugar and whisk vigorously until the mixture is pale yellow. Whip in the mascarpone until well combined. Gently fold in the egg whites until just combined.

5. Top the stout-soaked pound cakes in each jar with a few spoonfuls of the mascarpone filling, using up about half of it. Top the filling layer with another layer of pound cake, and drizzle each with another 2 Tbsp stout. Divide the remaining filling between the jars as the final layer. Dust the tops with cocoa powder, cover loosely, and refrigerate until well chilled before serving, about 2 hours.

OUR RECOMMENDED BREWS:

Bourbon County Coffee Stout GOOSE ISLAND / Victory at Sea BALLAST POINT / Imperial Eclipse Stout FIFTY FIFTY / Espresso Oak Aged Yeti Imperial Stout GREAT DIVIDE / Bomb! PRAIRIE ARTISAN ALES

MOLASSES STICKY TOFFEE PUDDING

DOPPELBOCK; OLD ALE; BARLEYWINE

THE PROPER MEANING OF "PUDDING" IS FAR FROM THE GOOPY CAFETERIA CUPS OF AMERICAN CHILDHOOD. The English describe pudding as an "extremely moist cake," and serve it in a variety of ways for dessert, often enhanced by the addition of a warm, sweet sauce. It's festive—ideal for holidays—filling, and rich, and its delicate, spongy texture inspires the clean-plate club.

In this version, the brown sugar–laced, treacly flavors and luxuriously silky, rich, toffeelike topping demand a big beer. By big, we mean high in alcohol, rich, boozy, warming, and substantial, but not too bitter. A well-brewed doppelbock (such as Ayinger's classic Celebrator) or a proper, not-too-hoppy English old ale or barleywine is the perfect foil for this rich, insanely satisfying dessert, matching sweet with sweet, roasty with roasty. If you have a fireplace to stoke in colder months, you've found the perfect dish to serve alongside it.

Makes 6 individual pudding cakes

PUDDING CAKES

4 OZ/115 G MEDJOOL DATES, PITTED AND COARSELY CHOPPED

½ TSP BAKING SODA

½ CUP/100 G FIRMLY PACKED DARK BROWN SUGAR

4 TBSP/55 G UNSALTED BUTTER, AT ROOM TEMPERATURE

1 TBSP MOLASSES

1 LARGE EGG

1 CUP/120 G ALL-PURPOSE FLOUR

½ TSP BAKING POWDER

¼ TSP FINE SEA SALT

MOLASSES TOFFEE SAUCE

1 CUP/240 ML HEAVY CREAM

¼ CUP/50 G FIRMLY PACKED DARK BROWN SUGAR

2 TBSP MOLASSES

¼ TSP FINE SEA SALT

1. TO MAKE THE PUDDING CAKES: Preheat the oven to 375°F/190°C. Butter and flour six cups of a standard muffin pan, tilting to coat evenly and dumping out the excess. (If the pan has additional cups, leave them empty.)

2. Put the dates in a small saucepan along with ⅔ cup/165 ml water and bring to a boil over medium-high heat. Remove from the heat and stir in the baking soda. Let stand for 10 minutes to soften and cool slightly. Purée the mixture in a food processor until smooth; set aside.

3. Cream the brown sugar, butter, and molasses on medium speed in a stand mixer fitted with the paddle attachment, or in a large bowl with a hand-held electric mixer, until the mixture is light and airy, about 5 minutes. Beat in the egg until fully combined. Sift the flour, baking powder, and salt into the bowl and mix just until combined. Gently fold in the date purée until fully incorporated, but avoid overmixing the batter.

4. Pour the batter into the prepared muffin cups, dividing it evenly and filling them about two-thirds to three-fourths full. Bake until they spring back to the touch and a toothpick comes out clean when inserted in the center, 15 to 20 minutes. Let the cakes cool for about 5 minutes in the muffin pan. While still hot, run a dull knife around the edges of each cake and invert the pan onto a wire rack to release the cakes. (Leave the cakes topside down to flatten the rounded edge as they cool.)

5. TO MAKE THE TOFFEE SAUCE: Combine the cream, brown sugar, molasses, and salt in a small saucepan and bring to a boil over medium-high heat. Cook, watching carefully and lowering the heat if it threatens to boil over, until reduced by half, 6 to 8 minutes. Remove from the heat.

6. Serve the cakes warm, topside down, on individual dessert plates. Spoon the toffee sauce over the tops, allowing it to drip down the sloping edges.

OUR RECOMMENDED BREWS:

Celebrator AYINGER / **Detonator** FISH TALE / **The Beer That Saved Christmas** PRAIRIE ARTISAN ALES / **Barrel-aged Human Blockhead** CONEY ISLAND / **Salted Caramel Stout** BREAKSIDE

CHOCOLATE SALAMI

BECAUSE THERE'S REALLY NO BETTER WAY TO END AN EVENING THAN WITH A PIECE OF CHOCOLATE AND A BOOZY-BEER NIGHTCAP, WE'RE SIGNING OFF THIS SHIFT IN THE BEER BITES KITCHEN WITH A PLAYFUL VISUAL RIFF ON A CLASSIC ITALIAN TREAT. Inspired by our friends at Olympia Provisions in Portland, Oregon—one of the nation's best producers of charcuterie, and chocolate salami, too—this edible optical illusion brings together complex flavors of quality chocolate, toasted nuts, candied ginger, and warm spices with imperial stout aged in Kentucky bourbon casks. The fine beer imparts deep layers of oak, vanilla, and wood. We were lucky enough to have a vintage bottle of Full Sail on hand (aged in Heaven Hill, Four Roses, and Makers Mark barrels), but any strong imperial stout (of 9 to 12% ABV) should be up to the task.

Makes two 8-in/20-cm salami

⅓ CUP/40 G HAZELNUTS, CHOPPED

¼ CUP/30 G SLIVERED ALMONDS

2 TBSP PUMPKIN SEEDS

4 OZ/115 G GOOD-QUALITY DARK CHOCOLATE (70 TO 75 PERCENT CACAO), CHOPPED

2 TBSP UNSALTED BUTTER

¼ CUP/50 G FIRMLY PACKED DARK BROWN SUGAR

2 EGG YOLKS

2 TBSP IMPERIAL STOUT OR CHOCOLATE STOUT

1 TBSP COCOA POWDER

½ TSP FINELY GRATED ORANGE ZEST

¼ TSP GROUND CINNAMON

PINCH OF GROUND CLOVES

PINCH OF FRESHLY GRATED NUTMEG

¼ CUP/20 G FINELY CRUSHED POTATO CHIPS

3 TBSP CHOPPED CANDIED GINGER

⅓ CUP/35 G POWDERED SUGAR

1. Preheat the oven to 350°F/180°C.

2. Spread the hazelnuts, almonds, and pumpkin seeds on a baking sheet. Bake until lightly toasted, 5 to 8 minutes, stirring once about halfway through. Set aside.

3. Fill a medium saucepan with about 1½ in/4 cm of water and bring to a boil over high heat. Lower the heat to maintain a low simmer. Place the chocolate and butter in a medium heatproof bowl and nestle it over the pot, making sure the water does not touch the bottom of the bowl. Leave it alone for 2 to 3 minutes to soften, then whisk until everything is fully melted and the mixture is smooth. Remove the bowl from the heat and set aside.

4. Meanwhile, whisk together the brown sugar and egg yolks in a medium bowl until smooth, then whisk in the stout, cocoa powder, orange zest, cinnamon, cloves, and nutmeg. Scrape in the melted chocolate mixture using a rubber spatula and whisk to combine. Add the toasted nuts, potato chips, and candied ginger and fold it all together until evenly distributed. Cover and refrigerate the mixture until semifirm, 20 to 30 minutes.

5. Lay out two 12-in/30.5-cm squares of wax paper on a clean work surface. Divide the chocolate mixture in half and place one half in the center of each piece of paper. Working with one at a time, fold the paper around the chocolate and mold it into an 8-in/20-cm log, rolling and squeezing it into an even width. Wrap the "salami" up tightly in the paper and twist the ends to seal. Refrigerate until firm, at least 4 hours.

6. Spread the powdered sugar in a long pile in the center of a third sheet of wax paper and, one at a time, roll the salami in the sugar to coat; pick up the paper by the edges and use it to roll the salami around. Brush off the excess sugar to get the effect of a thin coating of white mold on the outside (like meat salami). For an extra-realistic look, you could tie the salami up in butcher's twine.

7. Serve the salami on an attractive cutting board, cut into thick slices. (The chocolate salami will keep in the refrigerator, wrapped tightly, for up to 2 weeks, or in the freezer for up to 2 months.)

OUR RECOMMENDED BREWS:

Bourbon-Aged Imperial Stout FULL SAIL / **The Abyss** DESCHUTES BREWERY / **Parabola** FIRESTONE WALKER / **Imperial Stout** AMAGER BRYGHUS / **The Angel's Share, Bourbon Barrel** LOST ABBEY

INDEX

C

D

V

Van Roy, Jean Pierre, 100

Vegetables. *See also individual vegetables*

    Fried Pickled Vegetables with Homemade Ranch Dip, 32–33

    Raclette with Roasted Root Vegetables, 96

Vienna Lager, 16, 36

W

Waffles, Raspberry Liège, 62–63

Water, 14

Wee heavy, 145

Weizenbock, 16, 60

Welsh Rarebit, Stilton, with Fig Jam, 125

White IPA, 16, 79

Wild and sour ales, 64

Witbier, 16, 46, 49, 50

Wright, Mike, 106

Y

Yeast, 14

Z

Zucchini, Chicken, and Peach Kebabs with Mint Salsa Verde, 57–59

ACKNOWLEDGMENTS

This book wouldn't be here without the vision of Bill LeBlond and Diane Morgan, who brought the idea to us and inspired us to make it our own and have fun in the process. We're grateful for the support, tenacity, and insights of Alia Habib, our literary agent and a beer lover herself. To the team at Chronicle Books, especially our sharp-eyed editors Sarah Billingsley and Doug Ogan and designer Alice Chau, thank you for turning our words into such a fine book. And much gratitude to photographer John Lee and food stylist Lillian Kang for bringing the recipes to life.

We're so thankful for the companionship and unflagging support of the lovely Lila Martin, our biggest cheerleader and a keen taste tester, who offered moral support and invaluable feedback throughout the writing (and eating and drinking) process. We're also grateful for our families for always encouraging us to pursue our dreams. Last but not least, to the many brewers, importers, bottle-shop owners, and other beer industry members we approached for advice, samples, and more samples (you know who you are!), thank you. This book is for you.